Raising Test
Using
nent

William L. Callison

ScarecrowEducation
Lanham, Maryland • Toronto • Oxford
2004

Published in the United States of America
by ScarecrowEducation
An imprint of The Rowman & Littlefield Publishing Group, Inc.
4501 Forbes Boulevard, Suite 200, Lanham, Maryland 20706
www.scarecroweducation.com

PO Box 317
Oxford
OX2 9RU, UK

British Library Cataloguing in Publication Information Available

Library of Congress Cataloging-in-Publication Data

Callison, William L.
  Raising test scores using parent involvement / William L. Callison.
    p. cm.
  Includes bibliographical references and index.
  ISBN 1-57886-122-5 (pbk. : alk. paper)
  1. Education—Parent participation—United States. 2. Home and
school—United States. I. Title.
LB1048.5 .C36 2004
371.19'2—dc22

                                        2003026422

⊗ ™ The paper used in this publication meets the minimum requirements of
American National Standard for Information Sciences—Permanence of Paper for
Printed Library Materials, ANSI/NISO Z39.48-1992.
Manufactured in the United States of America.

Life is a work of art, designed by the one who lives it.

Contents

Foreword

It is very difficult to find a book that is a valuable resource to both parents and program staff. This book seems to have it all! It offers advice, provides guidance on how to be successful, and tells how to avoid the pitfalls that are out there waiting for parents and staff alike. For both, this book is exactly what you may be looking for to use as a guide.

As you will soon find, this book is relevant, up-to-date, and offers a wide range of topics that includes all aspects of parent involvement moving from prekindergarten through high school. The author, Dr. William Callison, a professor of educational leadership at California State University, Fullerton, has been the director of a parent education program for Head Start at the national level and offers expertise my colleagues and I have found most valuable in our work with parents.

The reader will find concrete hints on what to do and what to avoid. Suggestions are offered that will increase all parents' abilities to be more successful helping their children prepare for and succeed in school. The theme of the book is the research that shows conclusively that parent involvement at home in their children's education improves student test scores and overall achievement more than any other factor, including the socioeconomic status of the family. That is why the programs for parents that I direct spend so much time and energy focused on parents and the way they interact with their children.

Parents are given suggestions for working with teachers and administrators as they give input in areas including curriculum and instruction, testing, preschool and family literacy, homework, father involvement, and reducing the use of alcohol and drugs. Suggestions are made about how to help with fund-raising, assessing and evaluating both programs and student progress, and how to interpret and use that information after it is gathered for future decision making. Many chapters provide case studies and research-based concepts with practical guides for implementation. Rarely does one book cover all the aspects of constructive parent involvement in school life.

The author's experience and expertise are clearly evident in this valuable resource handbook. This is a book that parents and school administrators need to have on their bookshelves ready to refer to on a daily basis. In addition to the research-based material found in this book, there are suggestions for application and implementation of the content. I know that I want to be first on the list to get a copy of this book for my professional library and am proud to have been able to read an early transcript and to offer my recommendation of the book.

Jan Hensley, director,
Bakersfield City School District
Family Literacy Program and
former elementary school principal

Preface

This book is intended to help parents guide their child toward improved school performance, personally and academically. My approach is based on a model developed by the National Parent Teachers Association titled National Standards for Parent/Family Involvement Programs. The standards include communicating, parenting, student learning, volunteering, school decision making, and advocacy and collaboration with the community.

As you consider the many suggestions in this book, you may find a decision model developed at Stanford University[1] to be helpful. The model's elements are Frame, Alternatives, Information, Values, Reasoning, and Commitment. These elements are like the links in a chain. The decision is only as strong as the weakest link. Each link can be considered from a "head" perspective and a "heart" perspective. A good decision makes sense and feels right. We can describe the strength of each link on a scale from 0 to 100 percent. One hundred percent is not perfection; it is the point where additional improvement isn't worth the effort or delay.

Helpful Frame: "The Best Way to Look at My Decision May Not Be What First Comes to Mind."

Framing is clarifying the situation we're going to solve. By situation, we mean the problem or opportunity that gives rise to the need to make a decision.

For example, you may want to help your child improve his reading speed because you remember that you could read more rapidly than he does when you were in the seventh grade as he, John, is. You talk to his teacher and she agrees he is among the slower readers in his class. She thinks he is not trying hard enough and is constantly daydreaming and bothering other students nearby. One of your friends has recently seen a PBS special on the work of Dr. Mel Levine, a pediatrician, and suggests you contact him at the University of North Carolina Medical School through the website www.allkindsofminds.org. You do that, and since you live in Southern California, he refers you to Dr. Rita Peterson at the University of California at Irvine. You make an appointment to see her and she gives John some tests. You are quite surprised to learn that she thinks his problem is an inability to pay attention and focus.

Creative Alternatives: "There's Usually a Better Alternative."

An alternative is one of the possible courses of action available to you. Now that you think that Dr. Levine and Dr. Peterson may have an insight you had not considered, you decide to talk to the principal of John's school about having several teachers attend "Schools Attuned" training at UC–Irvine next summer. Many people wrongly assume that they have few or no alternatives. Usually, there are many more potentially desirable alternatives than appear at first glance.

Useful Information: "Think and Learn About All Possible Outcomes and Their Probabilities."

Information means anything you know, would like to know, or should know that might influence your decision. At UC–Irvine, John's teacher learns about working with students whose electrons in the brain do not perform just right and they find ways to provide instruction that will allow them to begin to catch up with other students in their class.

Clear Values: "What Is Truly Important for Myself and Others, Now and in the Future?"

The values that are most important to a person can make a big difference to his or her decisions. Too often, people make poor decisions by overemphasizing the short term (e.g., cut down on TV) and underemphasizing the long term (e.g., support teachers to learn to deal with learning difficulties).

Sound Reasoning: "Before Deciding, Check My Reasoning with Someone Who Sees Things Differently."

Reasoning is how a person combines alternatives, information, and values to arrive at a decision. It is my answer to "I am choosing this alternative because. . . ." For important decisions, just saying "I am choosing this alternative because it feels right" is not enough. Sound reasoning requires an explanation, or rationale. For example, "I am choosing this alternative because it is better for people I care about than the other alternatives available. Here are the specifics . . . [alternatives considered, information taken into account including risks, values and trade-offs considered, method for combining these to arrive at a chosen alternative]."

Poor reasoning leads to poor decisions. For example, people frequently assume the upside and ignore the downside (e.g., "John will mature and learn to pay better attention next year when he gets a teacher he likes").

Commitment to Follow Through: "Living My Decisions Makes Them Real."

Commitment to follow through means a person is set to follow through and have the ability to do so in a purposeful manner. If we are only half-hearted about our commitment, our follow-through is usually less intense and may not achieve the best results.

Commitment to following through is like pulling an internal switch — after the switch is pulled, we do whatever it takes to make our decision real. When we shift from considering a decision to being in the state of commitment, we are clear and can proceed without reservation, conscious of potential consequences.

Successful follow-through requires resources such as time, effort, money, or help from others. It also requires being prepared to overcome obstacles. For instance, the teachers may not be willing to give up a week of their summer vacation to learn about Schools Attuned. In that case, you might have to pay an expert for individual help.

Process for Difficult Decisions: "Good Decisions Are Made One Step at a Time."

The way we go about making a choice may shape the choice that we make. It is in our nature to do what we know how to do. However, that may not be what is needed to reach the best decision. A good decision process will help us face whatever it is that is most important to reach the best choice, even if it is expensive and time-consuming. There is important new research indicating that parent involvement improves student test scores and academic performance.[2]

In this book, we encourage you to use this decision approach as you look at a variety of ways parents can help improve their child's academic and personal school performance. To give you an opportunity to try this model, please turn to appendix A, and select one of the one hundred ways to improve parent involvement in your child's school. Use several other suggestions from the list until you have memorized the approach and can apply it to approaches that you think might be helpful as you read the book.

NOTES

1. Ron Howard, www.decisioneducationfoundation.org, accessed July 7, 2003.

2. Anne T. Henderson and Nancy Berla, "A New Generation of Evidence: The Family Is Critical to Student Achievement," ERIC Identifier ED375968, 1994.

Acknowledgments

The National Standards for Parent/Family Involvement Programs used as the conceptual model for each section of the book is excerpted with permission from *National PTA's National Standards for Parent/Family Involvement Programs*, copyright 1998.

Many names have been changed to protect the confidentiality of proposals written by the author for school districts.

My thanks to Bernard J. Herman and Geri Marshall Mohler, professors at California State University at Bakersfield, for writing chapter 18, "A California Community Comes Together Working to Solve the Problem of Illiteracy."

Margaret Thompson authored chapter 21, "The Skagit County Best PLACE Collaboration." She has been the director of this $19 million effort funded by the 21st Century Fund of the U.S. Office of Education.

Introduction

The starting point for the organization of this book was a list of domains developed by the National Parent Teachers Association (NPTA) in 1998.[1] These domains represent ideas that are key for the success of parent involvement in education, and they are numbered 1 through 6 by the NPTA in order of their importance to parents and schools. The chapters in this book are grouped under these six domains. In this introduction, I will present each of the domains and explain how each chapter relates to it.

DOMAIN 1: COMMUNICATING—COMMUNICATION BETWEEN HOME AND SCHOOL IS REGULAR, TWO WAY, AND MEANINGFUL

(Communication is the foundation of a solid partnership. When parents and educators communicate effectively, positive relationships develop, problems are more easily solved, and students make greater progress. Too often school or program communication is one way without the chance to exchange ideas and share perceptions. Effective home–school communication is the two-way sharing of information vital to student success. Even parent–teacher conferences can be one way if the goal is merely reporting student progress. Partnering requires give-and-take conversation, goal setting for the future, and regular follow-up interactions.)

Chapter 1: Family–School Partnerships

One of the new developments in parent involvement is a focus on family–school partnerships. Many resources are available to provide parents and school staff help in developing a partnership. One option many parents who work with school staff put in place is a compact, described in the chapter. Other key ideas include strengthening family–school partnerships through good communication and mutual responsibility for children; providing before- and after-school learning activities for children; making effective use of facilities schools, community buildings, churches for children and families; giving parents the resources, training, and information they need to help children learn; offering teachers and principals the tools they need to engage families; and removing barriers that prevent some parents from becoming involved in their child's school.

Chapter 2: The Importance of Two-Way Communication

Schools should promote two-way (school-to-home and home-to-school) communication about school programs and students' progress. Staff at Riley School indicate that two-way communication with parents is a major reason for the school's success. Riley posted excellent scores on the Statewide Academic Performance Index. This chapter describes research on parents communicating with their children, using a case study of the Riley Elementary School in California. This school has focused on reading and language arts improvement, and it has made excellent use of a support teacher program, implementation of whole-language approaches to learning, and parent involvement to dramatically improve student performance.

Chapter 3: Establishing a Plan to Develop a Parent Scorecard Using Benchmarking

This chapter focuses on benchmarking, a process that helps parents gather the information they need to begin serious discussions with the staff at their child's school about ways they can help the school. An example of the benchmarking approach appears in this chapter.

DOMAIN 2: PARENTING—PARENTING SKILLS ARE PROMOTED AND SUPPORTED

Parents are a child's life-support system. Consequently, the most important support a child can receive comes from the home. School personnel and program staff support positive parenting by respecting and affirming the strengths and skills needed by parents to fulfill their role. From making sure that students arrive at school rested, fed, and ready to learn to setting high learning expectations and nurturing self-esteem, parents sustain their children's learning. When staff members recognize parent roles and responsibilities, ask parents what supports they need, and work to find ways to meet those needs, they communicate a clear message to parents: "We value you and need your input" in order to maintain a high-quality program.

Chapter 4: Parent Involvement and Academic Performance

Parent involvement is a critical dimension of effective schooling and positively impacts children's academic performance. In this chapter, the term *parent* refers to any caregiver who assumes responsibility for nurturing and caring for children, including parents, grandparents, aunts, uncles, foster parents, or stepparents.

Chapter 5: Father Involvement and Student Achievement

This chapter explores the role of fathers, who specifically can be a positive force in their children's education. The points made here should encourage fathers to become more involved in their children's schools and encourage schools to welcome fathers' involvement.

Chapter 6: Parent Involvement in Preschool and Family Literacy

Involving parents in supporting their children's education at home is not enough. To ensure the quality of schools as institutions serving the community, parents must be involved at all levels in the schools beginning with preschool. It is especially valuable if there is a family literacy component.

DOMAIN 3: STUDENT LEARNING—PARENTS PLAY AN INTEGRAL ROLE IN ASSISTING STUDENT LEARNING

Student learning increases when parents are invited into the process by helping at home. Enlisting parents' involvement provides educators and administrators with a valuable support system, creating a team that is working for each child's success.

The vast majority of parents are willing to assist their students in learning, but many times are not sure what assistance is most helpful and appropriate. Helping parents connect to their children's learning enables parents to communicate in powerful ways that they value what their children achieve. Whether it's working together on a computer, displaying student work at home, or responding to a particular class assignment, parents' actions communicate to their children that education is important.

Chapter 7: Strategies to Improve Parent Involvement: Lessons from California

Parents and school staff are interested to know how other schools have used parent involvement to raise test scores and improve instruction. The ideas are taken from an article by Jessica Garrison, an education writer for the *Los Angeles Times*. Garrison asked California principals of schools that had raised their scores using parent involvement approaches how they did it.

Chapter 8: School and Home Collaboration to Increase Parent Involvement

We cannot look at the school and the home in isolation from one another. Families and schools need to collaborate to help children adjust to the world of school. This is particularly critical for children from families with different cultural and language backgrounds. This chapter uses Iowa Elementary as a school exhibiting excellent school–community collaboration.

Chapter 9: Helping with Homework after School

Parents may support a homework program because they want their children to succeed academically, to like school, and to develop good study habits. This chapter suggests a number of Internet locations for help.

DOMAIN 4: VOLUNTEERING—PARENTS ARE WELCOME IN THE SCHOOL, AND THEIR SUPPORT AND ASSISTANCE ARE SOUGHT

Literally millions of dollars worth of volunteer services are performed by parents and family members each year in the public schools. Studies have concluded that volunteers express greater confidence in the schools where they have opportunities to participate regularly. In addition, assisting in school or program events/activities communicates to a child, "I care about what you do here."

For parents to feel appreciated and welcome, volunteer work must be meaningful and valuable to them. Capitalizing on the expertise and skills of parents and family members provides much needed support to educators and administrators already taxed in their attempts to meet academic goals and student needs.

Although there are many parents for whom volunteering during school hours is not possible, creative solutions such as before- or after-school "drop-in" programs or "at home" support activities provide opportunities for parents to offer their assistance as well.

Chapter 10: Being a Parent Volunteer

School staff need to help parents become successful volunteers, especially for at-risk students at the elementary level, where help can make such a difference. This chapter considers the factors that make a successful relationship between the parent volunteer and the school, such as the parent's personality and communication style, experience in working with children, and the school's goals.

Chapter 11: Volunteer Activities That Increase Parent and Community Involvement

Creating a school environment where parents and community members feel welcome and the need to provide support for all students so that a shared vision can be fulfilled involves planning and collaboration among all stakeholders. When each member of a school community understands their responsibility to our children, powerful students emerge from powerful schools.

Chapter 12: Preschool and Parent Mentoring Proposal

This chapter describes a project in the Agape Unified School District to enhance preschool programs. Parent mentoring plays a significant role in the program.

DOMAIN 5: SCHOOL DECISION MAKING AND ADVOCACY—PARENTS ARE FULL PARTNERS IN THE DECISIONS THAT AFFECT CHILDREN AND FAMILIES

Studies have shown that schools where parents are involved in decision making and advocacy have higher levels of student achievement and greater public support. Effective partnerships develop when each partner is respected and empowered to fully participate in the decision-making process. Schools and programs that actively enlist parent participation and input communicate that parents are valued as full partners in the educating of their children.

Parents and educators depend on shared authority in decision-making systems to foster parental trust, public confidence, and mutual support of each other's efforts in helping students succeed. The involvement of parents, as individuals or as representatives of others, is crucial in collaborative decision-making processes on issues from curriculum and course selection to discipline policies and overall school reform measures.

Chapter 13: Making Decisions about Testing

This chapter describes the factors that can lead to a greater understanding of the political concepts that affect school organizations and specifically the role testing plays in them, including influence, control, attitudes and feelings, trust, discontent, and dissatisfaction.

Chapter 14: Parent Involvement Using Shared Decision Making

Comprehensive parent involvement treats parents as stakeholders. Parents are involved in key decisions and attend relevant staff meetings, which leads to improved student achievement.

DOMAIN 6: COLLABORATING WITH COMMUNITY— COMMUNITY RESOURCES ARE USED TO STRENGTHEN SCHOOLS, FAMILIES, AND STUDENT LEARNING

As part of the larger community, schools and other programs fulfill important community goals. In like fashion, communities offer a wide array of resources valuable to schools and the families they serve. When schools and communities work together, both are strengthened in synergistic ways and make gains that outpace what either entity could accomplish on its own: Families access community resources more easily; businesses connect education programs with the realities of the workplace; seniors contribute wisdom and gain a greater sense of purpose; and, ultimately, students serve and learn beyond their school involvement.

The best partnerships are mutually beneficial and structured to connect individuals, not just institutions or groups. This connection enables the power of community partnerships to be unleashed.

Chapter 15: Fund-Raising and Writing Proposals

Most schools are looking at creative ways to conduct fund-raising. This chapter discusses several issues around the topic, including how much, how often, and how to determine needs and, further, how to share control. Creative ways of gathering resources are described, with examples.

Chapter 16: Online Parent University Proposal

This chapter presents a proposal based on needs assessment data gathered in Duncan City School District.

Chapter 17: Lessons from Large-Scale Parent Involvement Efforts

Three national programs where parents have played critical roles are described in this chapter: Head Start Supplementary Training Programs in Providing Child Development Associate Competency Based Training; the Urban/Rural School Development Program; and the National Dropout Prevention Center at Clemson University, Clemson, South Carolina.

Chapter 18: A California Community Comes Together Working to Solve the Problem of Illiteracy

This chapter is about a California community (Bakersfield in Kern County) that has approached educational problems in a collaborative and unified way. Businesses, educators, and service organization representatives discovered solutions in the most unexpected places.

Chapter 19: How Parents Can Help Develop Safe Schools

A safe-school plan is an all-encompassing program that provides for the safety and security of students and educators. It is an ongoing, systematic, and comprehensive process that addresses both short- and long-term safety measures to eliminate violent attitudes and behaviors in the school. Its basic goal is to create and maintain a positive and welcoming school climate in which all members take pride. This climate is free of drugs, gangs, violence, intimidation, fear, and shaming.

Chapter 20: Helping People Change

In this chapter, a model is presented for helping parents, teachers, and administrators experience the change necessary to achieve their goals.

Chapter 21: The Skagit County Best PLACE Collaboration

The Best PLACE (People and Literacy Achieving Community Enrichment) program is an example of how key organizations within a community can work together to make a difference for children and their families.

NOTE

1. All domain contents are taken from the National PTA web page, accessed July 21, 2003, www.pta.org/parentinvolvement/standards/index.asp. Excerpted with permission from National PTA's *National Standards for Parent/Family Involvement Programs*, © 1998.

1

Family–School Partnerships

Family involvement in education contributes to students' achievement in school. When families are involved in children's learning, at school and at home, everyone benefits—schools work better, families become closer, and students improve academically. For these reasons, families and schools across the United States are partnering up to take mutual responsibility for children's learning.[1])

One of the new developments in parent involvement is a focus on family–school partnerships. Activities for parent involvement include the following:

- Strengthening family–school partnerships through good communication and mutual responsibility for children's learning
- Providing before- and after-school learning activities for children
- Making effective use of facilities schools, community buildings, and churches for children and families
- Giving parents the resources, training, and information they need to help children learn
- Removing barriers that prevent parents from becoming involved with their child's school

A PARENT–SCHOOL COMPACT?

Principals and teachers, parents and other family members, students, and community members all have roles to play in helping students learn and achieve standards of excellence. Each teacher should be asked to write a learning contract with each student about instructional expectations. In addition, a parent–school compact provides an opportunity to create a partnership with your school. A *compact* is a document that clarifies what parents and schools can do to help children reach high standards.

The family–school compact from Signal Hill Elementary School in Long Beach, California, focuses on improving students' academic achievement by setting high expectations for all students and for all of the school's partners. The compact is only one piece of a larger family–school partnership focused on shared responsibility. Notice how the commitments within the compact integrate the shared responsibilities of the compact into a cohesive plan of action.

Purpose of the Compact

Developing a partnership compact is good experience for any school. Putting ideas on paper will help focus your thinking and planning. As you develop and use your compact, remember that your best resources are the people around you—the teachers, school staff, parents, students, and community members who share your concern about the school and about student learning. Each person has something valuable to offer to the compact; it's up to you to discover the potential in your school community.

FOSTERING PARENT INVOLVEMENT

A good place to begin the family–school partnership is to document the barriers to parent involvement created by such factors as family structures (dual career, single parent, teenage parent) and family work schedules (full-time, job sharing, flex-time). Such documentation can be accomplished through parent–teacher conferences, telephone calls, or a short questionnaire.

Documentation of the barriers to parent participation can then be used to develop policies that are likely to work with the parent community. For example, more options may be needed as to when parent–teacher conferences are held (before, during, and after school), how they are held (face-to-face, by telephone, by computer, in small groups), or where they are held (at the school, in the home, at a neighborhood center, or at the parent's place of employment).

Recommendations for parent participation should take into account the resources and expertise of parents. Care should be taken to offer parents a range of support, partnership, and leadership roles. For example, parents can participate by preparing classroom materials, serving on a committee to select classroom equipment and materials, or becoming a member of a search committee to select personnel. Participation can even extend to parents' leading classroom activities in which they have expertise.

Teachers can include topics that relate to both classroom and family environments when they develop informational newsletters, public relations material, and parent meetings. Family strengths, parent–child communication, childhood stress, and in-home safety all have the potential to affect children's classroom behavior. Of equal importance is the effect of these topics on family well-being. Schools can meet their objectives and serve the interests and needs of families by offering information and educational programs that give parents practical suggestions on topics like these and others.

Communicate to parents at the beginning of the year about school policies and services. Inform parents about classroom goals for the year, and give a few examples of what children will be learning. Also let parents know about the frequency and nature of parent–teacher conferences (discussed in more detail later). Once conferences are set, keep a calendar of when, how, and where family contacts are to be made.

For some parents, education today is quite different from what they experienced two or three decades ago. Fear of the unknown may be one reason that parents avoid contact with their child's school. For other parents, school may be intimidating because it reminds them of an unpleasant school experience of their own. Empower parents with confidence by supplying them with a list of questions they can ask teachers throughout the school year.

Effective Parent–Teacher Conferences

Parent–teacher conferences are a valuable way to strengthen the compact or partnership between families and schools. Teachers should strive to create a comfortable conference environment in which parents feel free to share information, ask questions, and make recommendations. Schedule an adequate amount of time for the conference so that the parent does not feel rushed. Here are some other ways to share responsibility with parents during the conference:

- Allow parents to begin the conference by asking their own questions and expressing their own concerns is one way to convey respect for their input.
- If the conference is held at the school, point out to the parent the projects that involved his or her child.
- Begin and end the conference by noting something positive about the child.
- Ask open-ended questions ("How do you help your child with her shyness?") instead of yes or no questions ("Do you help your child with her shyness?").
- Communicate in a way that matches, yet shows respect for, the parent's background. Be careful not to make assumptions about a parent's level of knowledge or understanding, and avoid talking down to parents.
- Send nonverbal messages of respect and interest. Sit facing the parent, and maintain good eye contact. Put aside paperwork, and postpone taking notes until after the conference has ended.
- Instead of offering advice, ask the parent to share feelings and suggestions for addressing an issue. Then offer your own input as a basis for negotiation.
- Limit the number of educational objectives set during the parent–teacher conference to those that can reasonably be addressed in a specified time. Break each objective down into simple steps. Assign parents and teachers responsibilities for meeting each objective in the class and home. Plan a strategy for evaluating the objectives from both the parents' and teacher's perspective.

Follow up the parent–teacher conference with a brief note thanking the parents for their participation. This is also a good opportunity to summarize major points discussed during the conference.

NOTE

1. U.S. Department of Education, *Partnership for Family Involvement in Education* (Washington, D.C.: CD, 1999). The materials have been edited by the author.

2

The Importance of Two-Way Communication

This chapter presents research on the importance of parents talking—explaining, asking questions, and providing (positive) feedback to their children. It then offers a case study of the Greatwood Elementary School in California and its ten years of efforts to improve student performance and bring it up to the Foothill City Unified School District average, even though Greatwood has a greater proportion of disadvantaged students than the district has overall. The focus at Greatwood is on reading and language arts improvement. The support teacher program and implementation of whole language are likely reasons for the improvement. The Greatwood staff also dedicate much of their energy toward parent involvement.

The Academic Performance Index (statewide testing) results for 2000 at Greatwood continue to show the power of the parent involvement program begun in 1990:

- Percentage of students tested: 100%
- Statewide rank: Second of ten
- Similar schools' rank: Seventh of ten

RESEARCH ON PARENTAL INVOLVEMENT

An article by Paul Chance in the March 1997 *Phi Delta Kappan* discusses an intensive longitudinal study of the effects of parents' behavior on their children's intellectual development. Researchers indicate there are wide differences in the experiences parents provide their children. Surprisingly, the biggest variant is in the amount of talking to their infants that parents did.

The better educated a mother was, the more she spoke to her child. Welfare parents addressed an average of about 600 words per hour to their children, working-class parents directed about 1,200 words per hour to their child, and professional parents addressed more than 2,000 words per hour to their children. These differences were stable across time and were not attributable to the child's gender, the number of siblings, whether both parents worked, or the number of people present during observations.

The differences were qualitative as well as quantitative. Parents who talked more also did more explaining, asked more questions, and provided more feedback, especially positive feedback. Professional parents, for example, commented positively on their children's behavior ("That's right," "Good," etc.) an average of thirty times an hour. This was twice the rate of working-class parents and more than five times the rate of welfare parents. When low-income parents did comment on a child's behavior, they were far more likely to criticize than to praise. All the families were loving and showed sincere interest in their children's well-being. They simply interacted with them differently.

The differences in parental behavior were associated with differences in the infants' achievement. Those children whose parents talked a lot—providing lots of positive feedback, lengthy explanations, and so on—scored higher on an IQ test and on measures of vocabulary development at age 3. When twenty-nine of the children in the study were followed up in the third grade, the pattern of early parental behavior continued to predict performance on language and IQ tests.

Neither socioeconomic level nor race could account for the differences in intellectual accomplishments. In fact, the correlation between socioeconomic level and test performance declined from age 3 to grade 3, while the association between parental behavior and test performance remained strong. What matters, it seems, is not whether the parents are black or white, rich or poor, educated or uneducated; what matters is what they do—in this case, talking, explaining, asking questions, and providing (positive) feedback to their children. As you will see, they worked successfully on many related parent–child interaction tasks.

FOOTHILL IMPROVES READING

Foothill City Unified School District is the one of the largest school districts in the West. The ethnic makeup of the district includes Hispanics, Caucasians, African Americans, and Asians, as well as other ethnicities.

The purpose of the district's Master Plan for Categorical Programs is to provide a framework for making maximum use of categorical funds in order to have a significant, positive effect on the achievement of educationally disadvantaged youth, especially in the area of reading. The plan was developed by a forty-two-member task force, divided into five committees that were asked to address program, instruction, parent involvement, change, and evaluation issues.

The subcommittee for parent/community involvement was asked to look at and define types and amounts of parent involvement needed to positively impact student achievement and to define specific strategies for achieving parent involvement.

Parent Involvement Policy

The board of education adopted the following policy relating to parent involvement:

Establishing and maintaining a PTA program

Establishing and maintaining a school site and/or school advisory council where appropriate

Including parent participation in the program and curriculum development

Helping parents develop parenting skills

Providing parents with the knowledge of techniques designed to assist their children in learning at home

Promoting clear two-way communication between school and family about school programs and students' progress

Involving parents, with appropriate training, in instructional support roles at the school

Supporting parents as decision makers and helping them develop their leadership in governance, advisory, and advocacy roles

Establishing a parent center with materials and books for parent use

Developing a family support team to assist parents with resolution of
those home problems that interfere with student learning

Creating a home–school agreement delineating home, school, and
student responsibilities

Greatwood's primary focus from 1990 to the present is to improve reading. The school wants all students to become independent readers who
have a love and joy of all literature-based reading. The full implementation of all materials provided by the Houghton-Mifflin Literature series,
including listening, speaking, reading, and writing skills, in conjunction
with the language arts portfolios for each student, was very beneficial.

In addition, Chapter I and school-based coordinated money is used to
provide the Literacy Place reading program in grades 1 through 6. This
program helped accomplish the school's reading goals. Staff development
played an integral role as well.

GREATWOOD SCHOOL

Greatwood School was chosen a California Distinguished School in 1997–
1998. Many innovative programs have been implemented, including a very
comprehensive parent education program. The principle underlying the
parent educative component in the Master Plan is that parents and community play an essential role in the success of students, and the goal of the
plan is to actively involve parents and the community in the education of
students.

The Innovative Projects allowance is intended to promote program improvement as well as to give more local flexibility in providing Chapter I
services. Part of the innovation funds are used to encourage innovative approaches to parent involvement or rewards to, or expansive use of, an exemplary parental involvement program.

Greatwood School Parent Involvement Program

In 1990–1991, Greatwood School began to implement the District Master
Plan for Categorical Programs. The parent education program, which began at the same time, has many components:

- *First Grade Parent Club meetings.* Conducted by the reading support teachers, these monthly meetings are designed to instruct parents in language arts strategies they can use with their children at home.
- *Home–school agreements.* As part of the Master Plan, home–school agreements were designed to involve parents in taking an active role in their children's education and to take responsibility in ensuring their child's attendance and homework responsibilities.
- *Parent library.* With some of the Chapter I Innovation Funds, library books were purchased for check-out to parents of first- and second-grade students. These books are checked out on a weekly basis.
- *School Advisory Council, School Site Council, and Bilingual Advisory Council.* Councils are mandated for schools. These councils are in place and are very well attended. Also, they have representatives who attend the District Advisory Council on a monthly basis.
- *Parent volunteers.* Historically, Greatwood School has had a fair number of volunteers who give time within the classroom. The number of volunteers, although lower than ten years ago, is still relatively high, and volunteers are a viable part of the instructional program.

In 1991–1992, the parent education program expanded to include these elements:

- *Take-home computers.* This program targets second-grade students who have been involved in the reading support program. Parents and students are trained together in the use of the computer as well as the software that is provided. The computers are taken home during the student's off-track time. Older, inexpensive computers are utilized.
- *Family reading–style classes.* Held in the fall and spring, these classes are targeted for all parents and students. Parents are taught different ways of reading to their students as well as providing an environment conducive to reading.
- *Literacy/ESL class.* Many of Greatwood parents are semiliterate or illiterate. To compensate for this need, literacy classes are held for parents every Thursday from 10:00 to 12:00 at the Feldheym Library. Dr. Ann Freeman, director of the literacy program, conducts these classes. Also, ESL classes are held at the library on a weekly basis for parents who are limited-English-proficient.

- *CASA*. The Community and School Alliance (CASA) program is a joint effort between the community and the schools to generate grants for teachers for specific school projects. Greatwood has a CASA grant for kindergarten students that funds a listen-and-learn story tape project. Story tapes and books are sent home with students and checked out on a weekly basis.
- *The family support worker*. The family support worker is the liaison between community and school. He or she makes home visits and phone calls to families in "at-risk" environments.
- *The family support team*. This team consists of the program facilitator, vice principal, family support worker, counselor, Chapter I nurse, health aide, and sociological services worker. The family support team looks very closely at students in grades K, 1, and 2 who are referred by their classroom teacher because of absences, tardies, a need for glasses, assistance with homework, clothing needs, and behavior issues. The team provides a variety of family support assistance.
- *P.R.I.C.E.* This is a parent education workshop to help parents build their children's self-esteem and to give parents strategies in working with their children in the areas of discipline and self-esteem.

Monitoring Performance Results: 1992–1993

The third year of the pilot program encompassed program evaluation. Administrators took an in-depth look at the implementation of the reading support program and the whole-language program, sought ways to "fine-tune" existing programs, and explored dissemination-expansion of programs throughout the grade levels as well as bringing these programs into other schools.

Progress toward Meeting Three-Year Objectives

Continuous-Reading

Continuous-Reading is a set of materials published by Houghton-Mifflin (1990) that allows the school to implement its whole-language curriculum. Continuous-Reading is the reading portion of the program. There were 269 continuous students at Greatwood with pretest scores on the Individual Tests of Academic Skills (ITAS). ITAS is a standardized test given to assess achievement in reading, language, and mathematics. Their average pretest score in reading was 36.0. The average posttest score was 38.1, a gain of 2.1.

When one considers that Greatwood School's population is one of the most economically depressed populations in all of the West and that the large majority of students begin here with little or no exposure to books, these scores are remarkable. Furthermore, these students did not have the highly successful whole-language experience in kindergarten that this year's kindergarten had. We would expect even better results next year because of the kindergarten program.

When the program began, not many people thought the school could make this kind of progress because of the at-risk environment in the Greatwood area. The doubters included many teachers. There are no doubters anymore at Greatwood School, nor have there been for ten years. The Academic Performance Index results for 2000 at Greatwood continue to show the power of parent involvement.

Questionnaire

Presented here is the questionnaire Greatwood uses to encourage parent involvement.

Parent Involvement in Our School

Parent Name _____

Address _____ Telephone _____

Child's Name _____ Track and Grade _____

Indicate your response to each of the following statements by circling either yes or no.

1. Yes   No   There should be many school activities that involve students, parents, and teachers, such as reading enrichment programs and recognition assemblies to honor student achievement.
2. Yes   No   Parents should be encouraged to work in the school as volunteers.

3. Yes   No   Parents should supervise children with homework.

4. Yes   No   Parents should be able to schedule visits to the school during the day to understand the kinds of experiences their child is having in school.

5. Yes   No   Should there be parent education classes and opportunities to teach parents how to help their children benefit from school?

If yes, which would you like to participate in this year?

____ Parent Club Meetings
____ Parent Library Check-out
____ Take-Home Computer
____ Parent Advisory Committee
____ Classroom volunteer
____ Literacy classes
____ ESL classes
____ P.R.I.C.E.—self-esteem/positive reinforcement

Would you like to know more about access to services?
If so, please check those you are interested in.

____ Health
    ____ Shots
    ____ Physicals
    ____ Care of teeth
    ____ Care of eyes/ears

____ Sociological Services
    ____ Clothing/shoes
    ____ Emergency food
    ____ Housing
    ____ Counseling for parents/child

This questionnaire will play an ongoing role in Greatwood's programs. Extensive parent involvement will be continued at Greatwood and at other schools in the district.

3

Developing a Parent
Scorecard Using Benchmarking

Families provide the primary educational environment; parent involvement in their children's education improves student achievement. This chapter focuses on benchmarking, a process used in the business world that parents can use to gather the information they need to begin serious discussions with the staff at their child's school about ways they can help the school. Benchmarking bridges the gap between ideas and performance.

To use benchmarking, a school that has defined an opportunity for improved performance identifies another school (or program within its own organization) that has achieved good results and conducts a study of the other school's achievements and practices. The results are reported on a performance scorecard and circulated to parents, teachers, and administrators at the adapting school. The process then goes on to include the development and implementation of strategies that will help the adapting school improve performance. These benchmarks or lists are then used to prepare a parent scorecard.

BENCHMARKING DEFINED

Because of its focus on exemplary performance, benchmarking could be defined as locating and adapting best practices. Benchmarking is about more than discovering best practices, however. It includes comparative measurement, active goal setting, and implementation. A school staff might begin using benchmarking when they realize that they might not be asking the right questions about a problem or group of problems. For example, staff at Central Elementary School, located in the heart of a California city with boundaries including older-middle and low-income housing, wanted the school to improve in several areas (e.g., they were having difficulty getting parents to attend school activities designed for them). They thus began a benchmarking process for locating best practices, which led them to consider the program at Lincoln Elementary School, a few miles away.

The principal of Lincoln cited the campus's involved parents as a major reason for the school's success. Lincoln posted the highest gains of any school in the county on the state's new statewide index. When she arrived two years ago at the school, where most students are Latino, only a handful of parents were PTA members. Now there are 150. Hundreds more parents participated at the beginning of the year in seminars about the U.S. education system. And, with grants from the school and a private organization, parents have opened an off-campus center in a nearby apartment complex where children can go for help with homework.

Benchmarking helps organizations learn exactly where their performance lags. In this case, Central could compare its approach to parental involvement with another elementary school nearby that had far better results in this area. Let's consider now some of the specific elements that help Lincoln attain such success.

COMPARATIVE MEASUREMENT

The Lincoln Performance Scorecard starts with easily obtainable information about the school from the California Statewide Academic Performance Index (API). These results are from the Stanford 9 norm-referenced assessment that is administered in conjunction with the Standardized Testing and Reporting (STAR) Program. The API Base summarizes a school's performance on the 2000 STAR on a scale of 200 to 1,000 using national percentile rankings. The statewide rank of 10 is the highest and 1 the lowest. Each decile in each school type contains 10 percent of all schools of that type.

Similar schools are compared by pupil mobility, pupil ethnicity, pupil socioeconomic status, percentage of teachers fully credentialed, percentage of teachers who hold emergency credentials, percentage of pupils who are English language learners, average class size per grade level, and whether the schools operate multitrack year-round educational programs.

PRINCIPAL'S MESSAGE

The principal at Lincoln has clearly articulated the school's mission and goals:

Lincoln Elementary School is committed to provide an instructional program where every child achieves; where there is a clean, safe campus environment with a nurturing climate; and where there is a program that develops good citizenship and provides a strong foundation for further learning.

Lincoln Lions Love Learning! Achievement is the product of dedicated professionals, caring parents, and students who want to learn. Students, parents, and teachers are partners in a community that works together promoting individual growth and academic achievement.

Our curricular focus areas are mathematics and language arts. In mathematics, our students are developing mathematical skills. We provide experiences that stimulate students' curiosity and build confidence in investigating, problem solving, and communication. Students learn to listen, speak, read, and write through a language arts program that has its foundations in phonics, organized language skills instruction, and an overall emphasis in reading and writing the English language. Computer-assisted tutorials are available to all students in our state-of-the-art computer lab and classroom network systems.

Students learn best when faced with genuine challenges, choices, and responsibility for their own achievement. Those of us in the Lincoln Community provide opportunities for our students to engage in learning activities that spark genuine curiosity promoting the love of reading and writing.

PROGRAM HIGHLIGHTS

To master skills in listening, speaking, reading, writing, and mathematics, the following programs are in place at Lincoln:

Schoolwide Lincoln Lions Always Stop Everything to Read (L.L.A.S.E.R.) Program
English Language Learners (ELL) Center
Mathematics Competition (grades 4–5)
Literature Circles Reading Clubs
Intersession classes
Family Reading Night
Reading Is Fundamental (RIF)
Library
Multimedia center
Saturday school
After-school reading tutorials
After-school Math Club
Miller-Unruh reading specialist
Year-round calendar to support continuous learning

To develop self-discipline and motivate students for personal success, the following programs are available:

Schoolwide Discipline Plan
Peer Assistance Leadership (PAL)
Conflict resolution training
After-school Homework Club
Monthly awards and recognition
Caught-in-the-act cards
Student Council
Monthly Perfect Attendance Clubs
Counseling groups

To understand and appreciate individual talents and uniqueness, Lincoln students and staff participate in these activities:

GATE Program (grades 3–5)
Schoolwide music and art programs
School choir
After-school sports

CENTRAL ELEMENTARY'S USE OF BENCHMARKING

Central would like to improve its comparative measurement in two ways: by meeting it growth target and by improving its statewide rank. Approximately 1,200 students attend grades K–6, including students with special needs and physical and developmental challenges. Its diverse student population continues to grow and create an exceptional dimension to each child's education. At Central, individual differences are celebrated.

Central has few of the fine programs listed for Lincoln, but, with a list of them and descriptions of their features, it can employ a benchmarking approach and move toward improvement. A progress report is issued annually so that members of the local school community can be informed about and involved in the ongoing improvement of their school.

Active Goal Setting

Central exists for the parents and children of its community, and its staff believe the school can only get better if the community is involved and supportive of the ongoing changes needed to prepare children for the twenty-first century. School programs are reevaluated each year. Both teachers and parents are involved in looking at test results, analyzing the needs of our students and researching exemplary programs that could be implemented. This group also selects a focus area for the year; in 2001, this area was language arts with an emphasis on reading.

Central's Parent Leadership Council and Staff Leadership Team meet frequently to accomplish these goals. The School Plan includes high standards for student achievement, grouping strategies used by tracks and grade levels to enhance successful learning, a strong language development program, and multiple methods of developing student competence and self-esteem.

Implementation

Teacher-leaders in the areas of language arts, math, science, and technology disseminate information, assist in gathering materials, attend district trainings, and provide site in-services in their specific areas of strength. The two technology teacher representatives have been provided with mobile technology stations complete with hardware and software, compliments of the district. These representatives also receive training that enables them to lend technology assistance to their fellow teachers.

To successfully educate children, teachers need parental support. Last year over 90 percent of the Central parents participated in one or more of the parent education activities, including Family Math, Family Reading, Parent Institute, and Los Niños Bien Educados. In addition, the school offers English as a second language classes for parents on Monday and Wednesday evenings.

Just as students receive feedback on their progress, teachers receive regular feedback on their performance, too. Teachers are evaluated at least every two years; the purpose of evaluation is to promote quality instruction and improve the instructional process. Major areas evaluated are student progress, instructional practices, adherence to district curriculum objectives, discipline and control, and creation of a suitable learning environment.

Teachers are offered opportunities for professional improvement through the staff development program and individual assistance from curriculum specialists and mentor teachers. During the 2001–2002 school year, instructional support in language arts was provided through in-services on guided reading, phonics, phonemic awareness, literacy centers and flexible groupings, demonstration lessons, classroom visitations, and the new teacher academy. Instructional support for mathematics was delivered through publisher staff development sessions, district seminars, site-level in-services, demonstration lessons, and the new teacher academy.

All of Central's teachers have bachelor's degrees; 42 percent of the teachers, as well as the principal and vice principal, hold advanced degrees or are currently enrolled in advanced course work through local colleges and universities. All regular and special education teachers and support services staff are assigned in accordance with their credentials. Waivers are filed with the Commission on Teacher Credentialing if it becomes necessary to assign a teacher to a position outside his or her credential authorization due to the unavailability of personnel holding the authorized credential.

Central's improvement is no doubt due to several factors. However, the school's effective use of benchmarking, using a neighboring school as a basis for comparison, played an integral role.

4

Parent Involvement and Academic Performance

A critical dimension of effective schooling is parent involvement. The term *parent* refers to any caregiver who assumes responsibility for nurturing and caring for children, including parents, grandparents, aunts, uncles, foster parents, and stepparents. Many schools are now using the term *family involvement*. Research has shown conclusively that parents' involvement at home in their children's education improves student achievement. Furthermore, when parents are involved at school, their children go farther in school and they go to better schools.

This chapter focuses on the role of parents in helping their child succeed in school. Increasing evidence indicates that parent involvement increases test scores.[1] This means that teachers and administrators, who are under pressure to raise scores and may receive rewards if they do, are interested in parents contacting them and asking how they can help their child progress. New research indicates that family factors are more than eleven times as influential as school factors in predicting student performance in school.[2] We have an excellent opportunity to make changes based on experience in many schools that are dealing with the need to set high standards and institute programs that will be successful. This chapter will identify programs and strategies that are working.

We support raising standards where high levels of assistance are provided to staff, not the testing approach where students may be retained in grade because of a single test score. In the programs that are seeking to help students improve their performance in a variety of assessments, how did they get parents involved in a meaningful way? These will be described briefly here. Finally, this chapter will consider some of the real-world complexity that leads to successful programs and the language that communicates clearly to parents.

THE BIG PICTURE

Ronald Brownstein,[3] writing in the *Los Angeles Times*, sees four goals for improving schools:

1. Parents need to commit to helping their child's education through reading for fun every day, watching television less, discussing homework, and making reading materials available.
2. Title I, the federal program to assist low-achieving students, needs competition. It may spend too much on poorly qualified teacher aides and not enough on after-school programs, for example.
3. The states need a benchmark for judging student progress, since some states reduce their expectations to fit their student test results. Brownstein suggests we use the National Assessment of Educational Progress (NAEP) to keep state officials in line.
4. We need federal programs that are large enough in scale to make a difference. With many millions of students underachieving, programs to get better-trained teachers into hard-to-serve schools are critical.

WHAT IS PARENT INVOLVEMENT?

The National Coalition for Parent Involvement in Education (NCPIE) describes parent involvement thus:

> By exchanging information, sharing in decision-making, helping at school, and collaborating in children's learning, parents can become partners in the educational process. When parents/families are involved in their children's

education, children do better in school. Schools improve as well. (www.ncpie.org)

NCIEP also notes, "As the momentum for ongoing, organized family participation at the school and district level increases, so does the demand for family involvement program information." The following sections describe keys to successful programs as well as some specific program ideas.

DEVELOPING A POLICY FOR PARENT INVOLVEMENT

The process of developing policies should include community-based organizations (CBOs), teachers, administrators, business, families, students, and other key stakeholders.

Policy Checklist

- Opportunities for all parents/families to become involved in decision making about how the family involvement programs will be designed, implemented, assessed and strengthened
- Outreach to encourage participation of families who might have low-level literacy skills and/or for whom English is not their primary language
- Regular information for families about the objectives of educational programs and about their child's participation and progress in those programs
- Professional development for teachers and staff to enhance their effectiveness with families
- Linkages with special service agencies and community groups to address key family and community issues
- Involvement of families of children at all ages and grade levels
- Opportunities for families to share in decision making regarding school policies and procedures affecting their children
- Recognition of diverse family structures, circumstances, and responsibilities, including differences that might impede parent participation. The person(s) responsible for a child many not be the child's biological

parent(s), and policies and programs should include participation by all persons interested in the child's educational progress.

Keys to Success

- Assess families' needs and interests about ways of working with the schools.
- Set clear and measurable objectives based on parent and community input, to help foster a sense of cooperation and communication between families, communities, and schools.
- Hire and train a parent–family liaison to directly contact parents and coordinate family activities. The liaison should be bilingual as needed and sensitive to the needs of family and the community, including the non-English-speaking community.
- Develop multiple outreach mechanisms to inform families, businesses, and the community about family involvement policies and programs through newsletter, slide shows, videotapes, and local newspapers.
- Recognize the importance of a community's historic, ethnic, linguistic, or cultural resources in generating interest in family involvement.
- Use creative forms of communication between educators and families that are personal and goal oriented, and make optimal use of new communication technologies.
- Mobilize parents/families as volunteers in the school assisting with instructional tasks, meal service, and administrative office functions. Family members might also act as invited classroom speakers and volunteer tutors.
- Provide staff development for teachers and administrators to enable them to work effectively with families and with each other as partners in the educational process.
- Ensure access to information about nutrition, health care, services for individuals with disabilities, and support provided by schools or community agencies.
- Schedule programs and activities flexibly to reach diverse family groups.
- Evaluate the effectiveness of family involvement programs and activities on a regular basis.

WHAT PARENTS CAN DO TO HELP THEIR CHILDREN

This book is directed to all parents, regardless of income. Parents whose background is most like that of the teachers in a school may find it easier to relate to the teachers and other school staff and, consequently, to work with them. We are including examples of strategies for parents with backgrounds that are unlike the school staff's as well as those that are similar.

Parent efforts should be designed to accomplish the following:

- Help parents develop parenting skills to meet the basic obligations of family life and foster conditions at home that emphasize the importance of education and learning.
- Promote two-way (school-to-home and home-to-school) communication about school programs and students' progress.
- Involve parents, with appropriate training, in instructional and support roles at the school and in other locations that help the school and students reach stated goals, objectives, and standards.
- Provide parents with strategies and techniques for assisting their children with learning activities at home that support and extend the school's instructional program.
- Prepare parents to actively participate in school decision making and develop their leadership skills in governance and advocacy.
- Provide parents with skills to access community and support services that strengthen school programs, family practices, and student learning, and development.

These six types of parent involvement roles require a coordinated schoolwide effort that has the support of parents, teachers, students, and administrators at each school site. Professional development for teachers and administrators on how to build such a partnership is essential.

At the national level, the PTA has created a list of standards that can also help a group of parents as they prepare to have meaningful involvement in schools. There is an extensive overlap between the California State Department of Education's and the national PTA's guidelines, which includes the following five areas:

- Develop parenting skills.
- Use two-way communication between home and school.

- Involve parents in student learning.
- Assist in school decision making.
- Work with the community.

It is important that these objectives be seen in the context of programs that provide staff development and other kinds of support to teachers as they seek to improve student learning and also raise school test scores. To say it another way, parents should be careful to learn whether their child is attending a school where one test score can prevent their child from being promoted to the next grade or better, one where there are several assessments.

ISSUES FOR PARENTS TO NOTICE

Education is high on the national political agenda, and this is true for most states as well. Consequently, many governors and legislators are tempted to apply a "quick fix" for school improvement. The quickest way to improve scores is to focus entirely on test scores and not on the broader issue of improvement of instruction across the board. As in so many aspects of life, however, a quick fix does not last long.

The narrow focus is often called test preparation or "prepping." This name is associated with so-called prep or independent schools whose students often come from affluent families. These schools tend to focus on excellent instruction, and they use a variety of assessments to judge student performance.

The prepping at public schools is done after school or in other noninstructional time, typically. Consequently, parents who are not familiar with prep schools are led to believe that if their school focuses on narrow test preparation, they are like prep schools. This view could hardly be farther from the truth, and common sense would tell us that it is unlikely that well-educated, affluent parents would pay large fees for "quick fix" education that does not focus on problem solving, critical thinking, and other instructional approaches that are seen in a broad and powerful curriculum.

Another issue for parents to discuss with school staff is the use of tests in the school. Standardized tests, the kinds that states often require, are designed for comparisons of large groups of students. Some schools use the scores from these well-known tests to evaluate teachers and schools. For example, a realtor might suggest a parent would want to purchase a home in School A's attendance area, where the score on a statewide test is higher, than in School B's attendance area using just the particular state's systemwide score. A more knowledgeable comparison would use several variables, such as those described in chapter 3.

Another common mistake would be for a parent to ask that her child be moved from Miss Brown's room to Miss Black's room because she had seen that the reading, math, and language scores are higher in Miss Black's room. These required scores might hide the difference in the student backgrounds in the two rooms. Miss Brown may have many more students who do not speak English very well, for instance.

A FINAL WORD

Schools that undertake and support strong comprehensive parent involvement efforts, like those just described, are more likely to produce students who perform better than identical schools that do not involve parents.[4] Schools that have strong linkages with and respond to the needs of the communities they serve have students that perform better than schools that don't. Children who have parents who help them at home and stay in touch with the school do better academically than children of similar aptitude and family background whose parents are not involved. The inescapable fact is that consistently high levels of student success are more likely to occur with long-term comprehensive parent involvement in schools. Furthermore, research indicates that home–school collaboration is most likely to happen if schools take the initiative to encourage, guide, and genuinely welcome parents into the partnership.

The issue of parent involvement in the education of their children is much larger than improving student achievement. It is central to our democracy that parents and citizens participate in the governing of public institutions. In that respect, parent involvement is fundamental to a healthy system of public education.

NOTES

1. Anne T. Henderson and Nancy Berla, eds., *A New Generation of Evidence: The Family Is Critical to Student Achievement*, ERIC Identifier ED375968 (Columbia, Md.: National Committee for Citizens in Education, 1994).

2. Terry M. Moe, ed., *A Primer on America's Schools* (Stanford, Calif.: Hoover Institution Press, Stanford University, 2001).

3. Ronald Brownstein, "2 Gloomy Education Reports Should Serve as Guideposts for Reform Effort," *Los Angeles Times*, April 16, 2001.

4. Henderson and Berla, *A New Generation of Evidence*. This report covers sixty-six studies, reviews, reports, analyses, and books. Of these, thirty-nine are new; twenty-seven have been carried over from previous editions. An ERIC search was conducted to identify relevant studies. Noting that the most accurate predictor of student achievement is the extent to which the family is involved in his or her education, this report presents a collection of research papers on the function and importance of family to a student's achievement and education in school and the community. The research is divided into two categories: (1) studies on programs and interventions from early childhood through high school, including school policy, and (2) studies on family processes. The first category presents studies that evaluate or assess the effects of programs and other interventions, including early childhood and preschool programs and home visits for families with infants and toddlers, programs to help elementary and middle schools work more closely with families, and high school programs and community efforts to support families in providing wider opportunities for young people. The second category presents studies on the way that families behave and interact with their children, including the relationship between parent involvement and student achievement from the family perspective, characteristics of families as learning environments and their effects on student performance, and class and cultural mismatch. Major findings indicate that the family makes critical contributions to student achievement from the earliest childhood years through high school, and efforts to improve children's outcomes are much more effective when the family is actively involved.

5

Father Involvement and Student Achievement

Until recently, fathers were the hidden parent in research on children's well-being. Their importance to children's financial well-being was widely accepted, but their contribution to other aspects of children's development was often assumed to be secondary to that of mothers and was not usually examined. Reflecting this bias in research on child development, many federal agencies, and programs dealing with family issues, focused almost exclusively on mothers and their children. In 1995, President Clinton issued a memorandum requesting that all executive departments and agencies make a concerted effort to include fathers in their programs, policies, and research programs where appropriate and feasible. Research stimulated by the new interest in fathers suggests that fathers' involvement in their children's schools does make a difference in their children's education[1] (Nord, Brimhall, and West 1997).

Fathers can be a positive force in their children's education, and when they do get involved, their children are likely to do better in school. Unfortunately, many fathers are relatively uninvolved in their children's schools. Fathers are well advised to become more involved in their children's schools, and parents and educators should encourage schools to welcome fathers' involvement.

As noted in earlier chapters, children who have parents who help them at home and stay in touch with the school do better academically than children of similar aptitude and family background whose parents are not involved. The inescapable fact is that consistent high levels of student success are more likely to occur with long-term comprehensive parent involvement in schools. This involvement is a better predictor of school success than family income. The new research on the significance of specifically father involvement documents these assertions and is discussed in this chapter.

1996 NATIONAL HOUSEHOLD EDUCATION SURVEY (NHES: 96)

The NHES:96 was sponsored by the National Center for Education Statistics (NCES). The involvement of fathers in two-parent and in father-only families is presented and contrasted with that of mothers in two-parent and in mother-only families. Information related to the link between father involvement and student achievement is presented for children living in two-parent and in father-only households. (The analyses are restricted to children living with biological, step-, or adoptive fathers. Children living with foster fathers are excluded.)

The Extent of Father Involvement

Two-Parent Families

The proportion of children living in two-parent families with highly involved fathers is about half of the proportion with highly involved mothers: 27 percent and 56 percent, respectively. In other words, in two-parent families, children are twice as likely to have mothers who are highly involved than to have fathers who are highly involved in their children's schools. Nearly half of children in two-parent families have fathers who participated in none or only one of the four activities described earlier since the beginning of the school year. In contrast, only 21 percent of children living in two-parent families have mothers with such low participation in their schools.

Single-Parent Families

Children living with single fathers or with single mothers are about equally likely to have parents who are highly involved in their schools: 46 percent and 49 percent, respectively. Both fathers and mothers who head single-parent families have levels of involvement in their children's schools that are quite similar to mothers in two-parent families and are much higher than fathers in two-parent families.

Types of Involvement

In two-parent families, there are two activities for which fathers' involvement approaches that of mothers: attendance at school or class events (e.g., a play, science fair, or sports event) and attendance at general school meetings. Fathers may find it easier to attend these types of activities because they are more likely than the other two to occur during nonschool and nonwork hours. Fathers in father-only families are more likely than fathers in two-parent families to participate in these and other activities, so work constraints are not the sole explanation for low involvement among fathers in two-parent families.

FATHER INVOLVEMENT IN SCHOOLS

The following excerpt is from *Father Involvement in Schools*, a document prepared by the Educational Resources Information Center (ERIC), which details additional findings regarding fathers' role in their children's education.

Policymakers and educators agree that family involvement in children's education is closely linked to children's school success.[2] Many policymakers, school officials, and families, however, often assume that family involvement means *mothers'* involvement in schools is important. This assumption has some basis in truth in that mothers are more likely than fathers to be highly involved in their children's schools, and the extent of their involvement is strongly related to children's school performance and adjustment (U.S. Department of Education, 1997).[3] An important question, however, is, Does fathers' involvement matter as well? In two-parent households, do fathers make a contribution over and above that made by mothers? And in single-parent households headed by a father, does fathers' involvement in children's schools make a difference to children's performance in school?

This issue brief looks at the link between fathers' involvement in their children's schools and kindergartners through twelfth graders' school performance using data from the NHES:96, sponsored by the NCES. Information is presented for children living in two-parent and in father-only households.

The NHES:96 asked about four types of school activities that parents could participate in during the school year: attending a general school meeting, attending a regularly scheduled parent–teacher conference, attending a school or class event, and serving as a volunteer at the school. Fathers are said to have low involvement in their children's schools if they have done none or only one of the four activities during the current school year. They are categorized as having moderate involvement if they have done two of the activities. Those who have participated in three or four of the activities are said to be highly involved in their children's schools. (Not all schools offer parents the opportunity to be involved in each of these activities. Low involvement may be due to failure to take advantage of available opportunities for involvement or because schools do not offer parents opportunities for involvement.)

In two-parent households, children are more likely to do well academically, to participate in extracurricular activities, and to enjoy school and are less likely to have ever repeated a grade or to have been suspended or expelled if their fathers have high as opposed to low involvement in their schools.

Half of students get mostly A's and enjoy school according to their parents when their fathers are highly involved in their schools compared to about one-third of students when their fathers have low levels of involvement. . . . Students are also half as likely to have ever repeated a grade (7 percent vs. 15 percent) and are significantly less likely to have ever been suspended or expelled (10 percent vs. 18 percent) if their fathers have high as opposed to low involvement in their schools.

After taking into account such factors as mothers' involvement, fathers' and mothers' education, household income, and children's race/ethnicity, children are still more likely to get A's, to participate in extracurricular activities, and to enjoy school and are less likely to have ever repeated a grade if their fathers are involved in their schools than if they are not involved (U.S. Department of Education, 1997).[4]

After taking into account these other factors, mothers' involvement (but not fathers' involvement) is associated with a reduced likelihood of sixth through twelfth graders having ever been suspended or expelled.

In father-only households, children are more likely to do well in school, to participate in extracurricular activities, and to enjoy school and are less likely to have ever been suspended or expelled if their fathers have high as opposed to low levels of involvement in their schools.

Children living in single-parent households are, on average, less successful in school and experience more behavior problems than children living in two-parent households (McLanahan and Sandefur 1994).[5] Most research on single parenthood focuses on children living with single mothers. Children living in father-only households also do less well in school than children living in two-parent households.

Children in father-only households do better in school, are more likely to participate in extracurricular activities, enjoy school more, and are less likely to have ever been suspended or expelled if their fathers are highly involved in their schools than if they have only low levels of involvement. Nearly one-third of students get mostly A's when their fathers are highly involved in their schools compared to 17 percent when their fathers have low levels of involvement in their schools. Even more striking, only 11 percent of sixth through twelfth graders have ever been suspended or expelled when their fathers have high levels of involvement in their schools compared to 34 percent when their fathers have low levels of involvement in their schools. Although a similar pattern is observed for grade repetition, the difference between children whose fathers have high and low levels of involvement is not statistically significant.

Even after controlling for such factors as fathers' education, family income, and children's race/ethnicity, children do better in school and are less likely to have ever been suspended or expelled if their fathers have high as opposed to low levels of involvement in their schools.

CONCLUSION

The observed patterns of fathers' involvement in their children's schools, linked to family structure, are consistent with existing research (Cooksey and Fondell 1996) and with the notion that there is a division of labor in two-parent families, with mothers taking more responsibility for child-related tasks, whereas in single-parent families the lone parent assumes the responsibility. Fathers and mothers in two-parent families may be operating under the mistaken assumption that fathers do not matter as much as mothers when it comes to involvement in their children's school. The results also support research showing that single fathers and mothers are more similar in their parenting behavior than are mothers and fathers in two-parent families (Thomson, McLanahan, and Curtin 1992).

The low participation of fathers in two-parent families offers schools an opportunity to increase overall parental involvement. By targeting fathers, schools may be able to make greater gains in parental involvement than by targeting mothers or parents in general. This is not to say that schools should not continue to welcome mothers' involvement, but because mothers already exhibit relatively high levels of participation in their children's schools, there is less room to increase their involvement.

The involvement of fathers in their children's schools is also important for children's achievement and behavior. In two-parent households, fathers' involvement in their children's schools has a distinct and independent influence on children's achievement over and above that of mothers. These findings show that fathers can be a positive force in their children's education and that when they do get involved, their children are likely to do better in school.

NOTES

1. A. T. Henderson and N. Berla, *A New Generation of Evidence: The Family Is Critical to Student Achievement* (Washington, D.C.: National Committee for Citizens in Education, 1994).

2. Christine Winquist Nord, DeeAnn Brimhall, and Jerry West, *Fathers' Involvement in Their Children's Schools*, NCES 98-091 (Washington, D.C.: U.S. Department of Education, National Center for Education Statistics, 1997).

3. Winquist et al., *Fathers' Involvement in Their Children's Schools*.

4. S. McLanahan and G. Sandefur, *Growing Up with a Single Parent: What Hurts, What Helps* (Cambridge, Mass.: Harvard University Press, 1994).

5. Winquist et al., *Fathers' Involvement in Their Children's Schools*.

ADDITIONAL REFERENCES

Clinton, W. J. 1995. "Supporting the Role of Fathers in Families." Memorandum for the heads of executive departments and agencies. Washington, D.C.: U.S. Government Printing Office. June 16.

Cooksey, E. C., and M. M. Fondell. 1996. "Spending Time with His Kids: Effects of Family Structure on Fathers' and Children's Lives." *Journal of Marriage and the Family* 58, no. 3, 693–707. EJ 537 273.

Henderson, A. T., and N. Berla, eds. 1994. *A New Generation of Evidence: The Family Is Critical to Student Achievement.* Washington, D.C.: National Committee for Citizens in Education. ED 375 968.

McLanahan, S., and G. Sandefur. 1994. *Growing Up with a Single Parent: What Hurts, What Helps.* Cambridge, Mass.: Harvard University Press. ED 375 224.

Thomson, E., S. S. McLanahan, and R. B. Curtin. 1992. "Family Structure, Gender, and Parental Socialization." *Journal of Marriage and the Family* 54, no. 2: 368–78. EJ 446 994.

U.S. Department of Education. 1994. *Strong Families, Strong Schools: Building Community Partnerships for Learning.* Washington, D.C.: Author. ED 371 909.

6

Parent Involvement in Preschool and Family Literacy

Involving parents in supporting their children's education at home is not enough. To ensure the quality of schools as institutions serving the community, parents must be involved at all levels in the schools, beginning with preschool. Key elements of such involvement include the following:

- Interactive activities between parents and children
- Training for parents as the prime educators of their children
- Age-appropriate education for children
- Literacy training

In addition, many schools encourage parents to visit their children's classrooms, talk to teachers, and receive progress reports.

An extensive literature documents the powerful connection between efforts to improve the literacy of parents and those of their children. Much of this information has been gained by large studies of Head Start and Even Start children and their parents. The findings suggest that school administrators, especially those at the elementary school level, should seriously consider establishing family literacy efforts to improve the performance of elementary students. This benefit carries over into middle and high school as well. Family literacy programs help parents make great gains in self-confidence and lead to success in gaining and keeping employment. This chapter will describe such programs in further detail as well as those that encourage parental involvement in preschools.

DEVELOPING A FAMILY LITERACY PROGRAM

Parents who would like to see their school set up a family literacy program might use the following checklist from the National Center for Family Literacy website (www.famlit.org):

 1. Is discussion of family literacy needs, assets, goals, and available resources
    a regular part of the family partnership agreement process in your school?
 2. Is your program making active efforts to support children and families so
    that they participate in family literacy services with sufficient intensity
    and duration to make sustainable impacts?
 3. Does your program assess and keep track of the progress of families and
    children in terms of increasing confidence and competencies in family lit-
    eracy and emergent literacy?
 4. Are there identifiable gaps in family literacy services, missing connections
    among components, or is there a need to improve the quality of services?
 5. What are the educational and non-educational needs of families in your
    community?
 6. Have you completed a community or neighborhood assessment?
 7. What are the employment needs?
 8. What programs are currently addressing these needs?
 9. Are there gaps in service delivery or any duplication of services to families?
10. How would a family literacy program fit into your community network of
    family services?
11. What model best suits the needs of the community based on an
    assessment?
12. How will the model meet welfare reform requirements in your commu-
    nity/state?
13. What resources will be necessary to support this program?

The following list presents categories and suggested questions that will
be helpful to readers interested in setting up family literacy programs connected to preschools.

Program Outcomes/Evaluation

• What are the specific outcomes you expect for the family members
  who enroll in your program?

- How will you measure each outcome?
- Who will be responsible for data collection and reporting to funders?
- How will results be used with students, collaborators, others?

Collaboration

- What are the agencies that will assist in the delivery of services for your program?
- How will you increase the awareness of family literacy issues and this program's goals among your collaborative partners?
- What steps need to be taken to assure that your collaboration is an active partnership?
- What can be done now to lay the groundwork for continued funding? Expansion?

Management and Staff Selection

- Who are the key administrators (school, agency, business, etc.) that must buy into the program to ensure its success? How will they receive the necessary background?
- Has the program coordinator been determined or will that position be a newly hired one? (This needs to be determined as soon as possible.)
- What are the steps necessary in hiring staff for this program?
- How will the process differ from other hiring procedures? (Multiple funding support? Equity of schedules and pay?)
- How will you determine whether potential staff members are team players?
- How will the project coordinator be involved in hiring staff?

Site Selection

- What criteria will you use for selecting sites for the program? Do the key people at each facility have ownership?

- What needs to be accomplished to prepare the physical environment for the program?
- As you think of the basic components of family literacy (adult education, early childhood education, parent support, parent–child interaction), are there any needs that should be addressed in site preparation?
- What needs to be accomplished to assure the acceptance and support of other staff members at the facility?

Staff Development

- How will you prepare your staff for their roles in the program?
- How will you respond to ongoing staff development needs?

Program Planning

- How will team planning be encouraged? Does the budget accommodate time for weekly team planning for staff and home visits to families?
- How will you accommodate the interaction among all family literacy sites in your city?
- How will you determine the daily and weekly schedule of students and staff?

Transportation/Day Care/Meals

- What will be your students' needs in areas of transportation, day care and meals? How will the program respond to these needs? Funding?
- Which partners can work with the sponsoring agency in these areas?

Recruitment and Retention

- What are the recruitment strategies you plan to employ? How will your strategy fit with welfare reform strategies in your community?
- What will be the ongoing plan for recruitment?
- How will you inform "gatekeepers"?
- How will teachers be involved in recruitment?

Equipment and Materials

- What existing equipment and materials will be used?
- What needs to be ordered? Through what agency?
- What time frame should be established that assures delivery of materials and equipment prior to program opening?[1]

MODEL PROGRAMS

As you think about specific program needs, it may help to read about the excellent approach used for family literacy in the Bakersfield City (elementary) School District in Bakersfield, California. Needs assessment data gathered in Bakersfield City School District indicated a need for greater services for children from birth to five years old throughout the district. The district thus began to develop programs geared for children prior to kindergarten, with a focus on parent involvement, citing research about in-depth parent involvement improving children's academic performance.[2] The programs that have been developed in Bakersfield include Baby Steps and Daddy STEPS, Even Start, and the Career Ladder.

Baby Steps and Daddy STEPS

Baby Steps provides new parents with emotional support, a network of community based resources, essential developmental information, and parenting classes. Parents of newborns are greeted at the hospital with a "Welcome to Parenthood Kit" they find valuable.

Daddy STEPS is modeled after the nationwide "Boot Camp for New Dads" program. It provides bimonthly training sessions at hospitals, clinics, and school sites. It is conducted in Spanish and English.

Both programs provide home visits to help parents prepare for their job as the child's first and most influential teachers.

Even Start

Even Start is a federally funded program for three- and four-year-olds. It provides literacy training to improve the educational opportunities of children and adults by integrating early childhood and adult education and literacy with parenting education. The program builds on existing community resources to create a new range of services. With a family focus, Even Start has three interrelated goals:

- To help parents become full partners in the education of their children
- To assist children in reaching their full potential as learners
- To provide literacy training for parents

Qualifications

Families must have children age zero through seven. Parents must participate in the Kern High School District or Kern Adults Literacy Program. Families must be committed to stay with the Even Start Program for the entire year, and they must not miss more than three times a year.

Classes and Services

The following are offered for parents:

GED classes
ESL classes
Computer training
Parent and child education classes
Technology to link home and school learning
Educational field trips

Young children in Even Start benefit from child care that provides a stimulating, nurturing, and safe environment; specific early learning activities for children; trained staff in early childhood development; small group sizes; several opportunities for learning and socialization in a literacy-rich environment; early experiences that help get children ready for school; and educational field trips.

Families are provided with time to learn together, parent and child education and support groups, toy making and arts and crafts classes, school-to-home technology, regular Family Literacy Nights, home-based and structured educational activities.

Career Ladder

The Parent University is the cornerstone of the Bakersfield City School District Career Ladder program. The following courses are utilized:

Confident Parenting (a ten-week program in English and Spanish): This program is designated for parents who are interested in improving their parenting skills.

Developing Capable People (a ten-week program in English and Spanish): This program is designed for parents and school staff members. It teaches effective strategies and techniques to help reduce family conflicts, promote better family management, encourage children to be responsible for their actions, develop strong beliefs in personal capability, and communicate more effectively.

Los Niños Bien Educados (a twelve-week program in English and Spanish): This program is designed specifically for parents who are Spanish speaking and parents of Hispanic origin. It teaches a series of child management skills within a value system that is particularly Hispanic—raising children to be "bien educados." Traditional role, gender, and age expectations, types of cultural adjustments, and other issues pertinent to Hispanic parenting in the United States are covered.

Effective Black Parenting (a twelve-week program in English): This culturally sensitive program was developed specifically for African American parents. It teaches an achievement orientation to African American parenting, including the "Path to the Pyramid of Success for Black Children," special coverage of such issues as Pride in Blackness, and specific child management and communication skills.

MegaSkills (a ten-week program in English and Spanish): MegaSkills have been called the "inner engines of learning." They are qualities, skills, and attitudes needed for success. This program is designed to help parents help their children succeed in school and beyond by helping them learn the basic values, attitudes, and behaviors that determine success.

The Bakersfield district also offers courses in beginning and intermediate ESL, computers (including many applications such as Word and

PowerPoint) and the Internet, citizenship preparation, and GED classes. Once parents have reached this level of course work, they are ready for Developing a Career Ladder for Parent Volunteers/Paid Aides through the Online Parent University. This is a partnership between the Online Parent University and Bakersfield City School District, linking with the Nursing Program at Bakersfield College, the Early Childhood Program at Bakersfield College, the Child Development Program at Cal State Bakersfield, and the Nursing Program at Cal State–Bakersfield. All participating organizations provide mentors for the Mentoring/Employment Program for parents.

NOTES

1. Key references for additional materials: W. W. Philliber, R. E. Spillman, and R. E. King, "Consequences of Family Literacy for Adults and Children: Some Preliminary Findings," *Journal of Adolescent and Adult Literacy* 39 (1996): 558–65; National Center for Family Literacy, *Even Start: An Effective Literacy Program Helps Families Grow toward Independence* (Louisville, Ky.: Author, 1997); National Center for Family Literacy, *The Power of Family Literacy* (Louisville, Ky.: Author, 1996).

2. U.S. Department of Education, "Even Start: Evidence from the Past and a Look to the Future," Planning and Evaluation Service Analysis and Highlights, 1998; available: www.ed.gov/pubs/EvenStart/highlights.html.

7

Strategies to Improve Parent Involvement

Lessons from California

We believe that parents and school staff are interested to know how other schools have used parent involvement to raise test scores and improve instruction. The ideas in this chapter are taken from an article by Jessica Garrison, an education writer for the *Los Angeles Times*.[1] Garrison asked California principals of schools that had raised their scores using parent involvement approaches how they did it.

Garrison quotes Kris Powell, the Orange County education department's director of parent programs, as stating, "Schools are no longer saying, 'Oh, gee, we have back-to-school night, and our parents don't come. They must not care.' . . . They are finding ways to get parents in there." For example, Wilson Elementary School in Costa Mesa provides Spanish-speaking counselors to help immigrant parents who might otherwise be overwhelmed by cultural differences. At Madison Elementary in Redondo Beach, teachers serve dinner to families and then lend a hand as parents assist their children with homework.

Many parents who use Wilson's services find them very valuable. The ten-week Families and Schools Together (FAST) program is funded by both private grants and state funds. Maria Escobar, who emigrated from Mexico fifteen years ago, believes she and her husband learned to praise their nine-year-old son more and scold him less—"the American way," she said. In addition, Escobar has developed friendships with other Spanish-speaking mothers at Wilson for support. Together, the women volunteer to supervise school lunch periods. Garrison quotes another mom in the FAST program

45

as saying, "My children are happier with me because I am participating in their school."

Karla Wells, the principal of Lambert Elementary School in Santa Ana, credits the school's active parent involvement as a major reason for the school's success. In 2003, Lambert posted the highest gains of any school in Orange County on the state's new Academic Performance Index, described in chapter 3. When she arrived two years ago at the school, where most students are Latino, only a handful of parents were PTA members. In 2003, there were 150. Many more parents participated at the beginning of the year in educational seminars; and with grants from the school and a private organization, parents have opened an off-campus center for help with homework.

It was successes at schools like Lambert that first made officials pay attention to the link between involved parents and successful students, said Carol Dickson, a consultant on parent involvement at the California State Department of Education. For much of the 1970s and 1980s, administrators believed that socioeconomic levels were the single biggest factor in determining how well children did in school. But then educators began to look at schools in high-poverty areas that were succeeding and wondered what their secret was. The finding: "There was one thing that trumps socioeconomic factors, and that was parental involvement," Dickson said.

More studies were done, and by the early 1990s, many education experts were convinced that getting parents into schools was the modern form of campus medicine. Bringing about such a sea change in school officials' attitudes, however, did not happen overnight, especially among busy educators trained to believe that teachers know best about their students' education. In addition, many traditional ways of getting parents involved in school, such as the PTA, did not work with immigrant parents, who were alienated by the formal rules.

The first major move for change came in 1989, when the state boards of education adopted policies calling for schools to get parents involved. By 1992, many states laid out plans for how to do so.

Two years later, the federal government joined the game with the overhaul of the Title I program. From then on, schools receiving funds from the massive antipoverty program had to show that they had involved parents. In 1998, California state legislators passed a parents bill of rights, giving parents the right to visit their children's classrooms, talk to teachers, and receive progress reports. Also in 1998, Proposition 227 ended most bilingual education in California. Along with that came state funding to teach English to adults. Many districts used that money to start English classes for parents, which brought them into the schools.

In addition, California's Academic Performance Index (API), which ranks all schools according to how well students do on standardized tests and how much they improve from year to year, has spurred an outpouring of parent interest in the schools. API scores provide a concrete way for parents to evaluate their children's schools, which in turn motivates them to better understand and get involved in what is going on in the classroom.

All this was given an added push in 1999, when the state legislature authorized $15 million to copy a Sacramento Unified School District program statewide. The program, which began four years ago at the request of local religious leaders, pays teachers extra to go to the homes of students at lower-achieving schools, to help parents feel connected to school and understand how to help their children. Legislators also set aside $5 million to train parents to be involved in school. Sixteen schools in Orange County and 146 in Los Angeles received grants. Among them are Madison Elementary in Redondo Beach and Washington Elementary in Santa Ana. Six years ago, Washington began one of California's first comprehensive parent programs. Every morning, parents are encouraged to go to their children's classrooms for the first half hour and read to them, according to principal Robert Anguiano. The school also hosts family literacy nights, including workshops on poetry, opera, computer technology, and how to get children into college.

According to Garrison:

> Last summer, the school began offering English classes for parents. Teachers also ask parents to read books to their children and write about the experience. Then the teachers write back to the parents.
>
> "It's had a tremendous effect on the school," said campus parent coordinator Bertha Benavides. "We have hardly any discipline problems at school. Just opening the doors to the parents has enabled them to be aware of what's going on and test scores have gone up."

NOTE

1. Jessica Garrison, "Schools Get Creative with Parent Involvement," *Los Angeles Times*, January 31, 2001.

8

School and Home Collaboration to Increase Parent Involvement

We cannot look at the school and the home in isolation from one another; families and schools need to collaborate to help children adjust to the world of school. This point is particularly critical for children from families with different cultural and language backgrounds.

At Kansas Elementary, located in an affluent community, teachers serve dinner to families and then watch and offer tips as parents help their children with homework. Kansas has a very active PTA and also provides families with referrals for basic needs and community agencies, medical and Healthy Families insurance, referrals for individual and family counseling, and parenting education classes and support groups.

The school's Parent Involvement Plan states its missions as "to insure student success through strong families and a strong community." The plan also cites the following goals:

Provide Parent Education Opportunities Promote Ongoing Academic, Social and Emotional Success Provide Awareness and Access to Community and School Resources Build and Strengthen Parent Involvement in Our School and Community

HISTORY OF THE PARENT RESOURCE CENTER

In 1998, Kansas Elementary received a Healthy Start Grant that provided the school with a Parent Resource Center and a community liaison. The community liaison represents Kansas families at the Collaborative Council Meetings. Formed in 1993, and the collaborative has more than 160 community members on its council. It represents a strong partnership of service providers united in the belief that agencies working collaboratively, rather than in isolation, and providing integrated rather than fragmented services can more effectively assist families. Prevention, early intervention, and family crisis management are addressed by the community liaison's utilization of collaborative partners to link Kansas families with community-based services such as social services, affordable health and mental health care, employment/career counseling, legal assistance, and law enforcement personnel. In the 2002–2003 school year, 103 families received assistance from Kansas's Parent Resource Center.

The school also enjoys collaboration between local youth and community services, and the Probation Department provides a free comprehensive risk and resiliency assessment of all family members. There are also links to the community recreation department and the Boys and Girls Clubs.

Parent involvement has been important in making this an excellent school. In fact, it is a critical factor in the competition to become a Distinguished School. Six years ago, Kansas began one of the state's first comprehensive parent programs. As part of this program, parents are encouraged to go to their children's classrooms every morning for the first half hour and read to them.

To round out our picture of this school, look at the special programs that have been made available for students:

Red Ribbon Week
Career Day Activities
School Improvement
Schoolwide Title I
Philharmonic Program
Reading Is Fundamental (RIF)
After-school reading program
Title VII Family Literacy Grant
Family Reading Week
Kinder Caminata
Preschool story time
High school tutors

Peer assistance leadership
Drug Abuse Resistance Education (DARE)
PRIDE
Technology grant
Girl Scouts
Peer mediation
After-school Sports Club
Repertory theater
Family literacy
Family math
Fall Program
After-school Homework Club
Reading mentors
Winter Program
Patriotic Program
International Program
Breakfast Book Club
Junior Firefighter Program

One might ask how a school develops such a powerful parent involvement program. The basic strategies suggest that parents should:

- Read to the child at home
- Support the teacher at school
- Look at the child's daily assignments
- Check to see that all homework is done
- See that the child brings necessary supplies to school
- Have reading material in the home
- Talk to the teacher regularly

If the parent can make the additional time:

- Read to students in the child's classroom
- Support family literacy nights, including workshops on computer technology and how to get children into college

In turn, the school should offer English classes for parents if needed.

EFFECTIVE LEARNING GOES BEYOND SCHOOL

While involvement in school means children are learning directly from teachers, how well they learn in school is closely related to their home environment and out-of-school time. Parents should consider the following tips:

- *Set expectations and be clear about them.* Children learn better when they know what is expected of them, when expectations are high — but realistic, when they understand what the consequences are for not meeting expectations, and when parents focus on effort, not just results. Expectations such as attending school every day, completing homework, and reading regularly can all help contribute to more effective learning.
- *Provide structure and routines.* Children learn best when they have structure and routine in their lives and when parents monitor their activities. Regular mealtimes, regular homework times, adequate time for play, and clear limits on use of television and video games are all important factors in helping to provide structure and routine.
- *Provide learning opportunities outside school.* Learning doesn't stop when children end their school day. Children are constantly learning from the world around them. Providing different kinds of meaningful and fun opportunities to learn can help them. This can be done by having interesting books and magazines around the home, creating science projects in the kitchen, working together to fix things around the house, playing vocabulary and math games — the possibilities are endless!
- *Support children's learning.* Encouragement for children in the face of both success and failure, celebrating successes small and large, being present at school conferences and events are some of the ways parents and others can support the learning of children in their lives.
- *Create a positive climate.* A positive climate where children feel warmth, acceptance, respect, and support helps them be better learners. Ideas include catching them being good, putting surprise notes in their lunch or school bags, telling them regularly that they are loved, and listening to them without distractions from television or newspapers.

- *Model.* There is no more powerful teacher for children than the model provided by the important adults in their lives. Watching what their parents do teaches children what to do. When adults don't value learning, children won't, either. Adults model learning by reading regularly, showing children how they solve problems, and asking children's opinions.

Adults, especially parents, can have a significant influence on how children's nonschool environment and activities influence their abilities to learn. These six areas provide a place to begin.

9

Helping with Homework after School

Parents may support a homework program because they want their children to succeed academically, to like school, and to develop good study habits. We suggest a number of Internet locations for you to consider.[1] In addition, many parents like the idea of extended day activities because it relieves the "latchkey kid" syndrome by providing of after-school care under adult supervision. Appendix E describes a Homework Club you could propose to your principal.

Here are some homework tips:

- Meet with your children's teachers to find out what they are learning and discuss their progress in school.
- Increase your children's interest in homework by connecting school to everyday life. For instance, your children can learn fractions and measurements while you prepare favorite foods together.
- Set up a certain time of day that is dedicated to homework. Follow up with your children to be sure their homework is complete and turned in on time.

READING

Reading aloud to your child is one of the most important things you can do to help him or her to become a strong reader.

Educational software programs can help build your child's skills in phonics and in reading overall. The programs in Edmark's award-winning Let's Go Read! Series include extensive practice with phonics. They also provide beautiful interactive books and speech recognition with a microphone. (Your child reads to the computer, and it responds.)

Two other software programs designed to develop phonics skills are Kid Phonics 1 (which may also be found under the title Davidson's Learning Center Series Phonics 1) and Kid Phonics 2, both from Knowledge Adventure.

If you have concerns or questions about the reading curriculum at your child's school, make an appointment to talk to his teacher. Ask the teacher to describe her approach to reading instruction and why she prefers this approach. It may be that your child's school or teacher does not emphasize phonics instruction at all, or perhaps phonics instruction is given in first grade, while kindergartners work on other skills.

Bear in mind that different approaches to reading instruction work for different children. Some children thrive with a whole-language approach, others do better with phonics instruction, and many children do well when the two approaches are used together.

Finally, if phonics instruction is important to you, consider setting aside some time this year to talk to the first-grade teachers at your child's school. Consider which teacher's approach—both in reading and overall—would best suit your child, then write a letter to the principal requesting that your child be placed in that teacher's class for first grade.

WRITING

Many vocabulary-building books are available. Here are two to get you started:

- Fab Vocab! 35 Creative Vocabulary-Boosting Activities for Kids of All Learning Styles by Marguerite Hartill (for ages nine to twelve) features vocabulary exercises and activities to help children use and apply vocabulary words.
- Merriam-Webster's Vocabulary Builder by Mary Wood Cornog (for teenagers and adults) teaches over four hundred classical Greek and

Latin roots that can be used to analyze and understand many modern English words.

For more books, try a keyword search at an online bookstore, such as Amazon.com.

If your children would like to do their vocabulary work at the computer, here are two software programs you might like to explore:

- Davidson's Reading Blaster Vocabulary: 9–12 features game-oriented vocabulary practice with dozens of vocabulary lists for students in grades 4 through 9.
- Merriam-Webster's Vocabulary Builder (listed earlier in the books section) is also available in a CD-ROM version.

To see a review of either of these programs, try a keyword search for the title at Brainplay.com.

For a lighthearted, fun approach to vocabulary building, your children can "enroll" at Vocabulary University on the web. Try out the online vocabulary tests, play word-oriented games, and even get a diploma at "graduation"!

If you'd like to familiarize your older child with words commonly used on standardized tests, such as the PSAT and SAT, check out Adam Robinson's book, *The Princeton Review: Word Smart: Building an Educated Vocabulary.*

One of the best ways for kids—or adults—to improve vocabulary is to read! Encourage your children to read a variety of age-appropriate fiction and nonfiction books. For recommendations, visit a site such as Carol Hurst's Children's Literature Site. If you don't already have one, invest in a good dictionary. Then, when your children want to know the meaning of a word they've encountered in conversation, reading, or through the media, look it up together. You can set a good example by looking up new words that you encounter, too.

MATH

Two keys to math success are understanding math concepts and memorizing math facts for quick recall. It's good that your child seems to understand the math she is learning. Some multiplication facts are easier to remember with a few simple rules:

- Any number multiplied by 0 equals 0; any number multiplied by 1 equals that number.
- Any number multiplied by 2 is simply the number added to itself. (Your child can relate this to the "doubles" from addition: $2 + 2 = 4$; $8 + 8 = 16$; etc.).
- Any number multiplied by 10 is that number written with a 0 after it.
- Any number multiplied by 11 is that number written twice.
- The numbers in each answer in the "9's" table add up to 9; for example, $9 \times 5 = 45$; $4 + 5 = 9$.

With your child, make a multiplication table that features a 10×10 grid (100 squares); number the columns and rows from 0 to 9 along the top and side of the table. Fill in the facts that your child knows and can remember quickly. If he or she can master the 0's, 1's, and 2's tables, there are only twenty-eight facts left to learn. Mastering the 5's and 9's tables leaves only fifteen facts! Once you have narrowed down the number of unknown facts, you can work on learning those that remain.

One of the most tried-and-true methods for memorizing math facts is repetition. Practice multiplication facts frequently with your child; try to get him or her thinking about them and saying them out loud until they become second nature. Try flash cards (purchased from a study aids store or made at home from index cards) or multiplication workbooks that feature lots of practice problems.

Try to keep multiplication practice fun; one way to do this is to play games with flash cards. For example, try a variation of "War." You and your child each draw one flash card (question side up). The player whose card has the higher answer wins both cards, but the player must answer both problems to claim the cards! Or try using flash cards with a board game; to "earn" a roll of the dice, a player has to first correctly answer a multiplication problem.

Many children enjoy practicing math facts at the computer. Educational software programs can help your child understand math concepts and use math facts in problems, which may in turn help her or him remember the facts. Edmark's Mighty Math Calculating Crew uses "Virtual Manipulatives" to help children understand multiplication and division. Number

Heroes includes "Quizzo," a fun math game show that provides practice with math problems, including multiplication.

If, after practice, you still have a handful of "stubborn" facts your child just can't seem to memorize, it may not be a problem. As long as your child knows most of the facts, he or she can use reasoning to derive a few others. (For example, if one knows that $5 \times 5 = 25$, one can add another 5 to find the answer to 5×6.) However, if your child is forgetting enough of the facts to cause problems in math class, and additional practice doesn't help, you may want to contact his or her teacher to discuss the problem.

SCIENCE

There are many good science pages on the web. Some let children experiment with online experiments and activities, while others present information in the form of child-friendly text, pictures, movies, and so on. Many provide ideas and inspiration for science explorations away from the computer.

Here are some science sites a second grader might enjoy:

Science Made Simple
Zoom Dinosaurs
Worm World
The Edible/Inedible Experiments Archive
Volcano World Kids' Door
The Space Place
The Science of Sound
The Little Shop of Physics
Science Fair Project Resource Guide

Remember that websites often change, go out-of-date, or disappear altogether, and new ones are appearing every day.

SOCIAL STUDIES

There are probably fifty different ways to learn the names of the fifty states!

You and your child can spend time quizzing each other over a blank map of the United States, making up silly songs, rhymes, or chants that help you remember the location of each state. For example, "Maine's northeast of New Hampshire; New Hampshire's east of Vermont. Massachusetts is south of all three and has great seafood restaurants!"

Visit an academic supply store and look for large map puzzles of the United States to put together. There are also map activity workbooks and geography games. For example, Puzzle Maps U.S.A. provides a series of puzzles that ask children to identify the missing states.

If you'd like to read a related book with your child, try *Wish You Were Here: Emily's Guide to the Fifty States.* Part travel diary, part atlas, this account of a young girl's trip across the United States features easy-to-read maps and interesting trivia about each of the fifty states.

Educational software programs such as Complete National Geographic and Where in the U.S. Is Carmen Sandiego? can add excitement to the process of memorizing the states.

On the Internet, visit Funschool.com to play Where's That U.S. State? The GeoNet Game doesn't specifically target names of states, but it does provide interactive lessons about the places and regions of the United States.

FOREIGN LANGUAGES

All-in-One Language Fun (for ages three through twelve) from Syracuse Language Systems teaches two hundred words in French, German, Spanish, English, and Japanese. The program takes an immersion approach, teaching solely in the foreign language. This may sound intimidating, but it's actually a time-tested and effective way to learn. Children don't need to know how to read or write to use this program.

Many young children learn well through song, and Lyric Language: French (for ages three and up) from Penton Overseas takes advantage of this fact, teaching language with music videos in French. The program is also available in Spanish or German. Both programs offer games that reinforce the sentences and vocabulary learned.

If your child is musically oriented, try Lyric Language. If he's a prereader, or if you'd like to expose him to several languages, All-in-One Language Fun may better suit your needs. For independent reviews of both programs, visit Thunderbeam and Children's Software Revue. If you can't find these programs at a local store, you can order them directly from the companies or through a website such as Thunderbeam.com.

THE ARTS

Be sure to make a wide variety of art materials readily available. This can include anything from construction paper and crayons to "throwaway" items such as empty boxes. Encourage your child to stretch her imagination by letting her know that in art, there are no limits. Paintings of blue people dancing on purple grass under a pink sky are perfectly acceptable, wonderful expressions. Take her on a sketching expedition and show her that art is all around her. Point out the colors and patterns in flowers, grass, and clouds, and take turns sketching what you see. Try throwing an arts and crafts party for your child and her friends. For activity ideas, you can check out some arts and crafts books from your local library.

Finally, expose your child to the works of master artists by taking him or her to an art museum or gallery. You may want to buy a few postcards in the gift shop and make a game out of finding the paintings or sculptures on the cards. Keep the visit short. For many kids, an hour or so is long enough.

THINKING SKILLS

Beyond entertainment, computers can be used to provide powerful support for your child's learning and to extend his understanding of the world. Good software also presents a wonderful opportunity for you to become more familiar with your child's thinking and his development of problem-solving strategies.

Spend some time working with your child at the computer to help him get the most out of the experience. Research has shown that adult involvement can improve children's attention span, memory, and thinking ability. Ask questions and offer suggestions as you work through a problem together. Your child will learn from his exposure to a more experienced problem solver—you. By spending time with your child at the computer, you will also have a chance to evaluate the programs he's using and to make sure that he's spending some of his computer time really learning.

LEARNING STYLES

Children's learning styles vary widely. Traditionally, American schools have valued certain types of intelligence, primarily mathematic and linguistic.

Recent research into human intelligence suggests that individuals can be "smart" in more than one way and that human intelligence is actually made up of what educational psychologist Howard Gardner calls "multiple intelligences." Gardner's theory of multiple intelligences is one way to explain students' different learning styles. According to Gardner's theory, there are eight main types of learners:

- *Logical-mathematical* learners enjoy ordered activities such as number and pattern games, and they possess strong problem-solving and reasoning skills.
- *Linguistic* learners are sensitive to the meanings and sounds of words, and they enjoy learning through storytelling, wordplay, and creative writing.
- *Musical* learners relate well to the different aspects of music—rhythm, timing, and pitch—and enjoy learning through singing or playing musical instruments.
- *Spatial* learners process visual cues well and enjoy creating and studying visual art such as pictures, maps, puzzles, or diagrams.
- *Bodily-kinesthetic* learners communicate meaning and feeling through creative dramatics, athletics, and physical movement such as gestures and dancing.
- *Interpersonal* learners function well in a group setting, often as leaders, and are aware of the feelings and behaviors of others.
- *Intrapersonal* learners understand clearly their own feelings and motivations, and are usually self-motivated and independent.
- *Naturalist* learners analyze, categorize, and make use of the different features of the environment.

We don't know of any single test you can give your child to figure out which learning style he has. In fact, you probably don't want to place him in one category or another. Most children have not one learning style but strengths in several.

You can find many clues to your child's learning style in your own observations. Did your child talk early? Is he a natural athlete? Does he excel in math? You may also want to compare notes with your child's teacher.

For more information about the different intelligences your child may demonstrate, see the Family Education Network's Multiple Intelligences Survey.

GIFTED CHILDREN

Tutoring other students can give your child valuable experience sharing her knowledge with peers. The relationship can be beneficial to both tutors and tutees. If your child's teacher is looking for other ways to enrich her curriculum for highly capable students, she might want to look at *Curriculum Activities for Gifted and Motivated Elementary Students*, by Artie Kamiya and Alan J. Reiman.

In addition to increased responsibilities in the classroom, encourage your child to pursue projects on her own, outside school. These projects might involve independent research, learning a new skill or handicraft, or joining an achievement club. Taking your child to the library to research a subject that interests her—perhaps one that caught her attention in school—is a great way to foster an interest in independent learning. Taking a class together might be fun, too; try karate or quilting or cooking—whatever suits your fancy!

Technology can be a wonderful resource for gifted children. Both the Internet and good educational software provide many opportunities for independent research and learning. The following parent guidebooks may also help you foster your child's gifts:

Growing Up Gifted: Developing the Potential of Children at Home and at School, by Barbara Clark.

The Survival Guide for Parents of Gifted Kids: How to Understand, Live With, and Stick Up for Your Gifted Child, by Sally Yahnke-Walker.

HOMESCHOOLING

We don't know specific homeschooling curriculums well enough to recommend them, but we can point you toward some sources of information
to help you find the right curriculum for your needs and your children's.
You might find it helpful to read *Home Education Resource Guide*, by
Cheryl Gorder, or *The Homeschooling Handbook: From Preschool to
High School: A Parent's Guide*, by Mary Griffith. These books offer advice on choosing materials and creating an effective study program as
well as other topics such as learning styles and assessment techniques.
Debra Bell's *The Ultimate Guide to Homeschooling* covers these areas
and also lists other helpful print and online resources.

Fellow homeschoolers may be one of your best information sources,
and the Internet can help you find them. Numerous online sites feature articles, suggestions, or chat groups about homeschooling. These include
the National Homeschooling Association, which offers lists of support
groups, magazines, books, and organizations. (There is a charge for mem-
bership.) The *Homeschooling Magazine* offers homeschooling information and an online newsletter. To find additional sites, try starting at the
Homeschooling Zone's list of Internet Resources.

NOTE

1. See www.riverdeep.net/for_parents/for_parents.jhtml.

10

Being a Parent Volunteer

As we get used to the idea that parent involvement of a significant sort is one of the main ways, if not *the* main way, to improve student performance, it becomes clear that school staff need to help parents become successful volunteers. The big problem is the time it takes school staff to provide this service. An area of special need is provision of support for at-risk students, especially at the elementary level where help can make such a difference. It is of critical importance to the success of the program that the parent volunteer (PV) and the supervising staff member are able to have a comfortable working relationship. Other factors that are taken into consideration are the parent's personality and communication style, experience in working with children, and the goals of the school.

WHAT ARE THE DUTIES OF A PARENT VOLUNTEER?

Parent volunteers may have a variety of duties, including attending district training as a means of becoming familiar with selected programs where teachers can learn to use PVs. One may use the PVs in a small-group setting or in classroom presentations if the parent can handle this level of responsibility. Aside from district trainings, a PV will be expected to attend biweekly staff meetings for sharing of information, further training, and supervision. At the school site, a PV will need to be a Jack- or Jill-of-all-trades, possibly making home visits with families of at-risk students, referring students or families to community agencies, and participating in data collection for district research projects. Although not all PVs will need to perform all of these duties each week, the PV position is a challenging and exciting job requiring flexibility, adaptability, and social skills in addition to counseling skills.

THE INTERVIEW PROCESS

Volunteers should go through a formal process and be treated as if they were paid staff. The first step in becoming a PV involves filing an application with the district personnel department. The parent should present not only educational but pertinent unpaid/volunteer experience that indicates ability to work in the school situation for which she is applying.

The interview process usually consists of an initial interview with district staff to determine the applicants' experience, interest, and ability to undertake the role of parent volunteer. This interview is sometimes conducted by telephone. Interviewing can be very stressful, and staff should make every effort to make the process comfortable for parent applicants.

A second interview with principals and/or other school contact persons will then be conducted to determine an appropriate placement at the particular school site. In assigning a PV to a particular school or schools, many factors are taken into consideration. First, the PV and the supervising staff member must have a comfortable working relationship. Some schools are very familiar with the functions of a parent volunteer and have thoroughly integrated the programs into their system. Other schools may be in the early stages of fitting parents into their already full schedules. These factors will obviously have an effect on PV assignments. In the former case, an important question might be, How well does this candidate fit into the existing scheme at the school site? In the latter case, the more pertinent question may be, Does this candidate seem confident enough to implement a new program in our school in a somewhat independent manner? In all cases, it's important to place people in situations where they are most likely to feel comfortable and successful, and a genuine effort should be made to accomplish that goal.

TRAINING OPPORTUNITIES

Among the many offerings available from the staff, an opportunity for excellent training experiences is one of the most valuable. New and potential PVs in the district are offered free training in the rationale and implementation of several programs that are specially designed for easy implementation by a variety of educational staff. For example, a program that helps students (and teachers, parents, and others) to understand and accept their reactions to changes in their lives would be a good choice. It is important that the district identify a specific program that parents can learn to implement; otherwise, school staff will resist the use of PVs as too time-consuming. Another program parents might learn to implement would be one designed to assist students in developing more successful social skills.

In addition to the districtwide trainings directed at becoming comfortable with the PV curricula, training is conducted about working at a school site, such as conducting groups, managing discipline, and working as a team. Referrals and follow-up may also be shared on a regular basis.

Often PVs have areas of interest in which they possess a great deal of information and experience. In these cases, they are encouraged to share their expertise by conducting trainings for other staff members. PVs' input about areas of need for training will be essential to the staff providing training on the topics. As new and returning PVs become aware of their own training needs, they should mention these to the coordinator who schedules ongoing trainings.

WORKING WITH THE PARENT VOLUNTEER COORDINATOR

To operate this effort as a serious district program, a parent volunteer coordinator needs to be identified to provide support for PVs. Often this responsibility is added to an existing responsibility. The coordinator can be very helpful in preparing materials that will be used at the school site(s).

Also, parents in these roles should be treated as if they were paid staff. For example, the coordinator may remind PVs that absences should be excused in advance, just as they would be for paid staff.

MAKING CONTACTS AT YOUR SCHOOL SITE

When beginning as a parent volunteer, you may begin to feel as though you're the only person at school who doesn't know everyone else and what all the rules are. In fact, it is this very feeling, experienced by virtually every PV I've talked to, that prompted the writing of this chapter.

Perhaps the most important thing to keep in mind is that becoming a parent volunteer is a process and that all of your duties and skills will not need to be performed on your first day on the job. Former and current PVs have contributed their ideas to this manual in a sincere effort to make this process of "becoming" just a little smoother. The following are, for the most part, suggestions rather than rules of conduct. Anything that a PV really must do will be indicated in the text.

Having gone through the two-interview process, new PVs will be called by the coordinator with an offer of the position and information about the school site assignment(s) that seems most appropriate. Should you accept the offer and make the commitment, there will be a few simple administrative chores to attend to (being fingerprinted, having a physical exam, etc.). After that, you may want to call your new school to introduce yourself and set up an appointment to meet with the principal. The principal is a very important person with whom to establish a working relationship.

Another VIP at your site will certainly be the school secretary. When you are in need of office supplies, use of copiers, or student information cards (these have parents names, addresses, and home phone numbers), or when you have questions about how the school runs, the secretary will either know the answer or know where to find out. It's a good idea to introduce yourself or have yourself introduced to the secretary at the time you have your meeting with the principal. There may be some housekeeping issues concerning supplies or copying machine procedures that can be discussed at this early date that will help everyone to avoid confusion later.

Presumably, you will have met the contact person at your school during your second job interview. Shortly after accepting the PV position, set up another meeting with this contact person to learn how PVs are utilized at the schools and its goals for the current year. Usually, some rapport will have been established with this person during the interview process, and that meeting will serve to further your working relationship. This may be a good time to ask questions about students with whom you will be working and teachers who have or have not referred students. You also may want to find out what the space considerations are at your school and in which nook, cranny, or classroom you will be conducting your group sessions if you will have that type of assignment.

A school contact person will want to take you around and introduce you to teachers and students on your first day on campus. Others may wish to schedule a time during the school's staff meeting during which to introduce you to the staff en masse. Either of these methods is workable, but you may want to ask for some time at a staff meeting in the near future anyway, just to be sure that you develop a recognition factor among the teachers and other support staff.

Another reason to be introduced at a staff meeting is that this is a perfect forum in which you can give the school staff information about the PV program and the service that you will be providing for their students. Many schools in the district may have had PVs for several years, and their staffs still value a brief "refresher" on what is available to their students; other schools have had less contact with PVs and will need you to clarify why you're there. In addition, new staff are often unaware of the existence of the program and will want to know about the curricula. You may even want to get started obtaining referrals of students from teachers whom you talk to during this initial staff meeting, or perhaps announce your intention to send referral requests in the near future.

During these first few days, make a point of becoming "visible" at your school. Spend time in the staff lounge during recesses and lunch time, getting to know the teachers and letting them know you. Ask to observe in the classrooms or offer to make a classroom presentation about the PV program or to present an actual lesson from one of the curricula. Get information from teachers about what their concerns are with referred students. It's very helpful to let the teachers at your school know that you are there to provide them with a resource that, by helping their students feel better about themselves, may help them to achieve more in the classroom. A teacher's classroom is, to a certain extent, her or his domain, so it's wise to request observation time and offer support, rather than telling teachers what you are going to do.

PV ISSUES

What follows is a list briefly covering some common matters that arise for
PVs as they adjust to their assignments:

- *Who's the boss?* You may experience some confusion during the first
  days, wondering to whom you actually report. In all cases, the principal is the "commander in chief" of everyday school functions and
  administrative decisions. The principal may want to be informed by
  you of all phases of your work, or he or she may prefer that you work
  with another contact person and be updated on your progress through
  the contact. Principals are particularly interested in giving their approval to correspondence going from any school staff member (including PVs) into the community. Thus, permission letters sent home
  to parents of students to be included in your groups must be approved
  by the principal or by the person delegated this authority by the principal. In any case, such issues can be resolved early by asking about
  them during those first meetings with your principal.
- *Supervision.* You'll need to know not only with whom you'll be
  working closely but how often you'll meet. Some PVs have good results with a loosely structured format in which, when questions arise,
  the PV brings them to the contact person at the first convenient time.
  Others have found that, without regularly scheduled meeting times,
  they often go weeks without meeting to discuss questions and concerns about students, and important information is never shared. Because all school staff are very busy and time is in short supply, your
  contact person may not think to offer a regular meeting time for sharing concerns. If this type of support is helpful to you, you should take
  responsibility for requesting a regular meeting time. Most contact
  people will be willing to schedule this time with you, if you clearly
  express a need for regular consultation.
- *Supplies.* Art and other supplies can be very important parts of group
  and individual counseling sessions. Obtaining paper, crayons, scis-
  sors, and other supplies may seem difficult unless you know whom to
  ask. The place to start is probably with your school secretary. If the
  secretary is unable to help you, the principal will surely be of assistance. In this day of very tight budgets, your school may want you to

have a small budget from which you can purchase supplies, or you may be given access to a general pool of resources at the school. You should not need to purchase necessary items out of your own pocket. However, if there is a particular item that you have found useful in groups and that you would like to purchase and use with your groups at school, that is certainly permissible. Often the school will have some puppets, toys, and other items that you may be able to use in your groups. Letting the staff know that you are interested in trying activities that they have found useful may provide you with supplies and activities as well as strengthen the bond between yourself and the school staff.

- *Office machines.* Most schools have one room that contains the office machines that the whole staff uses for preparing lessons. It's important to keep in mind that you will need to do some advance preparation of activities for your groups and classroom presentations, and it will be easier for you to accomplish this task if you can schedule prep time during off-peak hours during the day. Before and just after school, and during lunch breaks and recess times are among the times of highest usage of copiers and other office machines by the teaching staff. If you can schedule yourself around those times, you're less likely to get "bumped" off of a machine.
- *Illness or absence.* It is very important to let the school staff know when you are ill or unable to work for any reason. Teachers and students need to be informed when groups will not be meeting at their regularly scheduled times. Confusion results from not informing the school and making certain that the people affected by your absence are told in advance. Such an oversight can have a very negative effect on a PV's credibility at school as well as on the PV's relationship with students. If absence is unavoidable, let the school secretary know and ask her to inform the people affected by your absence.

Parent volunteers do important work and invariably find great satisfaction in the role. Their interest in and commitment to the school will have a positive effect on their children's school performance as well.

11

Volunteer Activities That Increase Parent and Community Involvement

Carla J. Poellnitz

Creating a school environment where parents and community members feel welcome and the need to provide support for all students so that a shared vision can be fulfilled involves planning and collaboration among all stakeholders. When each member of a school community understands its responsibility to our children, powerful students emerge from powerful schools.

Providing teachers with specific activities that encourage parents to become active participants and observers in homework assignments has proved to be valuable in the district. As teachers set clear goals based on the school visions, the success of every student is a desired reality, not a dream. Training parents through educational activities like the ones presented here will assist teachers in making the first step in creating strong school and family connections. Specifically, this chapter describes a literacy campaign at an elementary school site, including parents' role in that program.

ACTIVITY DESCRIPTIONS

The most popular events at W. R. Nelson School, the school described here, included Dr. Seuss Day, Family Reading Night, and Author Day.

Dr. Seuss Day is a popular event that is celebrated in every classroom on the campus. Community members—retired teachers, district personnel, business partners, city officials, Tustin Rotarians, Tustin Public Schools Foundation board members—are invited to join students and staff in a day of reading to celebrate the works and creativity of the famous author. Students are provided with strong role models from the community through this event.

Family Reading Night provides families with an opportunity to learn strategies and techniques to increase reading skills at home. Some participants choose to go to various sessions to listen to outstanding literature read by members of the school staff, and others attend sessions that demonstrate how to use various strategies to increase comprehension skills in the individual student. Since this is a family event, it happens to be one of the most successful of the year. Parents enjoy sharing a night with their children and having the opportunity to participate in activities that will help improve their own reading skills.

The Tustin Public Schools Foundation and the Tustin Unified School District sponsor Author Day each year. At this time, authors visit the site to share their works with every student in the school. Students learn the writing process through the various presentations and the importance of persistence and determination when reaching for a goal. While it is imperative to provide strong, successful role models to the students, creating families that are literate and understand the power of reading is one of the school's primary goals.

Most of the specific activities include portions where parents should record their responses and observations regarding the specific nightly assignments. It is helpful if teachers prepare parent response sheets and include them with most homework assignments. Questions can be phrased so that responses can only be made by parents if they participated in the assignment and/or observed the student in the learning environment and asked questions regarding the concept being reviewed. Nelson's parent trainings were held at Back to School Night to inform parents about how to make good observations and use them to address student weaknesses and strengths.

One activity entitled "Golden Lines" required the parent and child to read a book together, choose their own favorite line or quote from the text, and then explain why the quote was chosen by the individual and what it meant to the reader. This was found to be one of the most effective activities. The parent responses gave the teacher insight as to the educational background of the parent(s) and some idea of the types of literature children were allowed to choose to read at home. Responses often revealed customs and detailed information on the cultural backgrounds of the students. Responses made by the teacher on the same page were sometimes prescriptions for more appropriate reading text, follow-up readings or activities, or questions that required the student or parent to move to a higher level of thinking or application of a skill.

All families participated in this activity, but those with limited English skills often were shy about responding to given questions. The English language and literacy coordinator at the school site helped translate instructions to families at Back to School sessions and during goal-setting conferences. Parents interested in learning English were provided with common responses in English and simple pictures to help them choose appropriate responses to describe the child's progress.

The second activity, "I Know a Star," was used from 1996 to 1997 and required that each parent visit the classroom to present their child to the learning community. Parents could share a story, photographs, events, or a video about the child. During that year, every family in the class participated in the activity. This activity helped the teacher and students learn something unique about each member of the class. It also assisted parents in feeling comfortable in the classroom community and helped them share a part of themselves with the community. Students learned patience when listening to parents from various cultures, and they learned to politely ask questions when they did not understand a word or the significance of a shared event.

A third activity used in grades 1 through 3 was developed to help parents learn how students could apply grade-level skills to everyday situations at home and in the community. The Monthly Math Madness assignment was sent home at the beginning of each month and listed a single math task for the students to perform each day. From this assignment, parents also received ideas on various ways to review math skills at home on a daily basis. This assignment also encouraged parents to send in suggestions for other tasks that they wanted to see listed for the following month. This activity actually demonstrated to parents how teachers used various tasks to address the standards and taught them how to create their own materials at home to assess student knowledge of required skills through fun and entertaining activities. Presently, this activity is being used in every first-grade classroom at the school site.

An activity that has been used in all primary grades K–3, and is now being used schoolwide at the Nelson School site in the primary grades, is the Poetry Book. This activity was created to give all families an opportunity to hear the child read regularly at home. Books containing poems collected throughout the year are kept by each child and sent home on a weekly basis. A parent response page in the book requires parents to comment on student reading skills and oral expression. This book has prompted parents to ask more questions about literacy during parent conferences, and it often encourages parents to request information on how children learn to read and what can be done at home to strengthen literacy skills. All students keep the Poetry Books for the entire year and read them weekly at home and at school. Teachers using the system have seen students master the concepts of rhymes earlier in the primary grades, and they noticed that children became more interested in checking out poetry books in the school and classroom libraries. Parents are in-serviced at Back to School Night on the advantages of positively interacting with the student when reading the book each week. Many parents with limited reading materials at home use the book to read aloud to students each night.

The Family Night Activity assignment was the last activity used. Once again, a parent–student response sheet was used in this homework assignment. A variety of monthly home activities are listed for parents and students to actively participate in on a weekly basis as a family. The student and parent choose one activity from the list and respond to questions that inquire about skills the students learned by participating in the family activity with the parent. Parents who showed limited understanding for these types of assignments complained about the amount of work required on their part in nightly responses to the homework assignments. Parents who participated in the training and responded regularly in the homework journals often read over their responses and asked more questions during goal-setting conferences. They inquired about appropriate prescriptions for their child and a clarification of what the district standards meant and how their child ranked in mastering each of the grade-level standards.

CONCLUSION

Communicating with parents about the child's learning regularly through activities that require parents and students to learn and work together encourages more parent involvement at home. When teachers create activities that require this participation, parents feel like an effective team member in the child's educational program.

12

Preschool and Parent Mentoring Proposal

This project grows from needs assessment data gathered in Agape Unified School District that indicates a need for preschool coverage throughout the district. There is, however, no space for such programs. Boys and Girls Clubs (B&GC) plan to use space and staff in the seven B&GC Centers in Agape, beginning with 120 children and their families in two of the seven centers. Over time, the program would expand to reach the approximately four thousand children per year who need the program. The district includes forty-five elementary schools, and B&GC will eventually link preschools to the kindergartens in each of them. Parent mentoring will be a key part of the program, as will health services for participating children.

Agape Unified School District has experience operating kindergartens, and the B&GC of Agape have long experience offering services to children in the community through the seven centers. We have recently been licensed by the state to operate preschools and have opened a model facility in the center of the city. We are especially pleased to have the support of the Departments of Child Development and Nursing at Agape College. We will provide new services (we are careful in this project not to budget for services that currently exist) in the areas of antitobacco training, family planning, prenatal care, parent (health) education, pediatric care, and early intervention services (focusing on disabilities).

This project focuses on other areas of services as well, including mental health, nutrition, dental, and vision services, with differing levels of training to provide support to low-income children and families. We see nursing students being utilized to deliver health services, provide prevention training, offer communications and technology training, and gather data and carry out program evaluations.

The Department of Child Development at Agape College will supervise a number of interns in the delivery of services to the parents of participating centers. We will create a comprehensive approach to early childhood that involves ensuring that critical program areas are supported and that services are comprehensive, of sufficient quality, and well integrated with each other. In particular, progress is needed on planning for the integration of health and early childhood education services.

Mission Statement

Enhance Capacities. Enhance the capacities of participating B&GC Centers and related kindergartens to develop strong linkages which will improve the environments—normative, family, social service, health care, child care—in which children are conceived and young children grow and develop.

Develop Systems. Develop a system of comprehensive, integrated, high quality early childhood and health services, including anti-tobacco services, in every participating Center and school.

Improve Accountability. Improve accountability and performance measurement to ensure that all public and private funds directed toward young children are achieving the desired outcomes in the Centers and linked schools.

Improve Job Training for Parents. Each B&GC Center will also begin offering Mentoring and Employment Training to the parents of the participating children. These services will be offered by the nearest community college, at first on a non-credit basis and later for credit. Students would initially complete their high school equivalency diploma and then begin work on their Associate of Arts Degree. We will place them in an appropriate level of employment at the earliest opportunity.

Program Outcomes

Health Services

We place a high priority on improving health services, especially those directed to low income children and families. We will increase the number of children who are provided immunizations and inhaled medications, as needed. The key institution in this effort is Agape College and its nursing preparation program.

Education Services

We will develop pre-reading and oral language skills and help children to use an increasingly complex and varied vocabulary. We will seek to help children develop and demonstrate an appreciation of books and, in the case of non-English background children, progress toward acquisition of the English language.

Related to this effort is our plan to create a health and education data base of participating children and their families. This in turn will become part of the Preschool Profiles, which will be updated two times a year.

Objectives

Screening and Assessment

Use of a Standardized Screening Tool for preschool children;
Use of a full Child Observation Record kit; and
Implementation of Lesson Plans including individualizing of instruction and daily notes to make up a comprehensive file.
Also
Daily monitoring of each center and classroom using a Health and Safety checklist; and
Evaluation of each classroom and outdoor play environment using the Early Childhood Environment Rating Scale.

Health

The Profiles will contain information about each child and her/his family's progress in anti-tobacco training, family planning, prenatal care, parent education, child care, pediatric care, early childhood education services, and early intervention services (focusing on disabilities). These Profiles will be updated at the beginning and end of each school year in Phase 1 of the project. More frequent updates may occur later in the Project.

Education

Develop phonemic, print and numeracy awareness;
Understand and use oral language to communicate for different purposes;
Understand and use increasingly complex and varied vocabulary;
Develop and demonstrate an appreciation of books; and
In the case of non-English background children, progress toward acquisition of the English language.

We will create the Preschool Mentoring Program. It will assist Preschool Parents from the B&GC Centers to prepare for, obtain and maintain successful employment and further education through job and personal development mentoring. Mentoring will be carried out by work-study students from community colleges that will help existing and new entry level employees move toward living wage positions.

As collaborative partners in the mentoring project, we will work with low-income families in the B&GC Preschool Centers in order to help parents:

Obtain a high school equivalency diploma

Obtain entry level employment

Reduce staff turnover

Increase training and experience

Support career development

Retain employment

Preschool will work with participating community colleges to see that a variety of faculty and students are recruited to provide the services listed above. A key concept will be "training of trainers" where more skilled individuals train those who are learning new skills and understandings. More specifically we will deliver the following services:

Anti-tobacco training is provided to children, parents and staff at B&GC Centers using staff from the Tobacco Use Prevention Program of the Orange County Health Care Agency;

Child Development and School Readiness services provided by faculty and students from Agape and Coastline Colleges to participants so they can attend needed education and training.

Family planning, early intervention, pediatric care and prenatal care are strengthened through parent training conducted by nursing faculty and students from Agape College to participants so they can attend needed education and training.

Parent and staff education is enhanced by adding options that lead to a career path, including opportunity to improve their English language skills, if needed, and to complete a high school equivalency program. We will work to develop cohorts of parents who can support each other in these classes. We will also create a Mentoring & Employment Program to provide group and individual help to these parents. The courses will be offered by the participating community colleges. Parents can enter an Associate of Arts program of interest such as the ones in Human Services at Agape College.

Later they can enter California State University Fullerton or California State University Long Beach State for courses in their areas of interest.

Early intervention services—so that children at risk of developmental delays are provided every opportunity to achieve their potential. Agape College and Cal State Fullerton would provide training related to serving the Developmentally and Emotionally Disabled.

Plan

We propose to conduct a multi-year, multi-phase project to expand services for Preschool children, parents and staff in Health and Educational Services as described above. We will begin with a Year 1, Phase 1 effort with demonstrations at two Centers in Agape. In Year 1, Phase 2, we will also create the Mentoring & Employment Program in both Centers.

Community College Involvement with Preschool Proposal

Overview:

It is proposed that a program be developed to offer training through Agape and Coastline College programs for Preschool children, their parents and their care givers. This would be done initially at the two B&GC Centers. Courses leading to a high school equivalency diploma or test of General Educational Development (GED) will be offered. Instruction in parenting would be offered by non-credit programs and health and early childhood classes would be offered by credit programs through Agape and Coastline Community Colleges.

Proposal

NON-CREDIT ELEMENT: Non-credit programs at the participating community colleges will be offered. They will present a program for Preschool parents leading to a GED and/or offer parenting classes. English classes would also be included. These classes will be bilingual as needed.

CREDIT ELEMENT: The two Community Colleges will be contacted where the pilot programs are to offer instruction in appropriate health care and early childhood education.

ENROLLMENT ASSUMPTIONS: It is assumed that the two Centers will enroll approximately 120 children in the pilot program. There would probably be at least one parent per child interested in taking the provided adult training (either basic education and/or health and childhood classes). In addition, a Mentoring & Employment Program for all Preschool parents. It will serve parents in class size cohorts of 25 and could eventually serve hundreds of parents.

It is estimated that about half of these parents would be interested in the GED program. About one-third of these parents would need English classes.

It is assumed all parents would enroll in parenting and child development classes. The two Community Colleges could offer course work in basic health care with special emphasis against the use of alcohol, drugs and tobacco. They would also offer work in Early Childhood Education.

FINANCES: While the Preschool Proposal Grant will cover administrative salaries and supplies, teachers' salaries would be paid for by the colleges and financed by their claiming of ADA reimbursements. This is more advantageous to the colleges than direct payment for courses from the grant.

Community Colleges' Credit Classes

AGAPE COLLEGE would be contacted to provide course work through its Human Services, Nursing and Psychology Technology Departments. These courses would carry college credit. They would be in the field of health care and alcohol/drug/tobacco. Topics such as the following would be covered in these classes; pediatric care, prenatal care, effects of alcohol/drug/tobacco use, and availability of health and social agencies to help parents.

In order to initiate the project as soon as possible, we propose to screen in children and parents in the participating Centers whom staff feel should receive priority attention in our areas of focus including: anti-tobacco, family planning, prenatal care, parent education, child care, pediatric care, early intervention services, early childhood education, special needs, learning, physical health, mental health, nutrition, dental and vision services.

Community and Parent Involvement

Agape B&GC have an Advisory Committee for the Family Center which will provide input from the community and parents to guide the Preschool Project. . . . In order to be sensitive to community cultural diversity and the needs of the various populations served by the Center a variety ethnic and income groups are represented.

Leverage of Financial and Community Resources

We are collaborating with many organizations in order to make this project possible. We have the physical space that is critical for operating a new system of preschools in the community. The Agape Unified School District has the interest and capability to link their kindergartens to our new network of preschools. Agape and Coastline Community Colleges will provide us with the dozens of students and faculty to help our staff operate this very important new network of preschools.

Program Evaluation

In Year 1, Phase 1 Preschool children will be evaluated using the FirstSTEP Screening Test for Evaluating Preschoolers, which uses such tasks as picture completion, visual position in space, problem solving and auditory discrimination to determine whether the child might have a disability. In Year 1, Phase 2 this would be followed by the High Scope Child Observation Record for Ages 2.5 to 6 years and, later, the Early Childhood Environment Rating Scale, a program evaluation tool. We would also use Preschool Performance Indicators such as those seen in Attachment A.

In Year 2, we plan to extend our services into Kindergartens in the participating school districts. Depending on school preferences, we might use the School-Age Care Environment Rating Scale, among others.

Parent Participants will be assessed to see to what extent English language competence, level of education, and job experience affect the levels of support needed to be successful in: 1) life skills; 2) self advocacy; 3)gaining employment; 4) retaining employment once achieved; and 5) moving to additional training and higher level income.

Evaluation will be an important function and an integral part of program implementation both on the formal and informal levels. The results based model will consist of the following ongoing steps:

Clarify the intent of the evaluation program as required

Design data procedures based on measurable outcomes

Collect data

Summarize, analyze data

Determine program results

Report data to specified audiences

Review and modify

The evaluation of all children in participating programs will utilize clear standards and focus upon both process (are the steps taken to achieve outcomes conducive to program success?) and product (how well is the program accomplishing its specified objectives?). Because the evaluation is designed to be cyclical, so as to provide continuous feedback to the program, it will provide a formative evaluation process.

We are particularly interested in improving the extent of classroom observation by Preschool teachers and the record keeping that allows teachers to have a clear idea of the experiences each child needs in order to succeed in Grade 1. We plan to recruit student interns from Agape Colleges, as needed, to help in this area.

Attachment A: Preschool Evaluation Priorities

Use of a Standardized Screening Tool;

Use of a full Child Observation Record kit; and,

Lesson Plans including individualizing and daily notes to make up a comprehensive file.

Also

Daily monitoring of each center and classroom using a Health and Safety checklist; and,

Evaluation of each classroom and outdoor play environment using the Early Childhood Environment Rating Scale.

Develop phonemic, print and numeracy awareness;

Understand and use oral language to communicate for different purposes;

Understand and use increasingly complex and varied vocabulary;

Develop and demonstrate an appreciation of books; and,

In the case of non-English background children, progress toward acquisition of the English language.

In addition to the preceding items, educational performance measures have been established to ensure children:

Know that letters of the alphabet are a special category of visual graphics that can be individually named;

Recognize a word as a unit of print;

Identify at least 10 letters of the alphabet; and,

Associate sounds with written words.

Health Requirements

Immunization requirements for school entry. Required for Kindergarten Entry:

DPT, DT, DTaP: 4 doses total, if last dose is after age 4

(5 doses ok regardless of age given.)

Polio: 2 doses total, if last dose after age 4

(4 doses OK regardless of age given.)

Administer inhaled medication to children in care as long as they follow the safety measures required in the new law. These safety measures have been adopted. They include written instructions from the physician, written authorization and instruction from the parent, proper training, and maintaining proper records.

In order to provide parents with a greater opportunity to become active participants in the area of Nutrition Services, a Parent Nutrition Assistant (PNA) program has been implemented. At the center level, each Child Development Supervisor appoints one parent as a PNA volunteer. The two main responsibilities of a PNA are 1) to bring nutrition information to the center level on a regular basis, and 2) to encourage and support nutrition-related activities at the center. Each PNA obtains information by attending regular meetings, and a nutrition course provided by a local community college for which they have the option of receiving college credit. This program is also open to all Delegate Agencies opting to participate.

Disabilities Service Area Plan

Staff and Interns will provide support, training, and services to children, families and staff with diverse needs.

Children with Speech & Language impairments, Learning Disabilities, and those requiring Mental Health services continue to be the largest area of special needs. There has been a noticeable increase in the number of children with "autistic like" behavior identified under the Speech & Language category.

Attachment B: Training Outlines and Course Listings

Healthy Children—Training Outline
Early and regular assessment (of deficits and capacities)
Early health intervention—at risk, special needs, for ALL
Substance abuse reduction (ATOD)
Medical/health care home for all children
Healthy/safe environments
Access/expanded pre-natal care
Immunization
Increased breast feeding
Availability of health/nutrition education
Reduce preventable causes of:
    Death/infant mortality/injury
    Disability/chronic illness
    Child abuse/neglect; domestic violence
Informed & Responsible Parenting—Training Outline
Community-based, seamless system of support
Crisis intervention/prevention
Housing
Parents as advocates/families in charge
Comprehensive/quality parent education
Access to family planning
Increased family self-sufficiency/poverty reduction

Access to healthy family activities

Success in School—Training Outline

Universal screening and follow-up

Quality, compensation, affordability and professional status for early education providers/teachers

Track achievement in K–12 system of early childhood program graduates

Early care/education

Families in need

Strengthen quality of early education

Accreditation

NAEYC

Support parent empowerment/education

Literacy

Information

Increase family/non-traditional child care providers

Centralize child care/education coordination/system

Attachment C: Job Descriptions

Job Description for Project Director

1. To manage the Project and see to the implementation of the Goals and Objectives.
2. To help ensure timely performance of all aspects of project contract.

Job Description for Associate Project Director

1. To assist in the management the Project and see to the implementation of the Goals and Objectives, especially as they pertain to personnel and budget.
2. To help ensure timely performance of all aspects of project contract.

Job Description for Associate Project Director

1. To assist in the management the Project and see to the implementation of the Goals and Objectives, especially as they pertain to education and evaluation.
2. To help ensure timely performance of all aspects of project contract.

Job Description for Project Coordinator

1. To coordinate the Project and implement the Goals and Objectives.
2. To serve as liaison with the Project Director to ensure timely performance of all aspects of project contract. Measure: Print out lists of tasks to be accomplished and indicate levels of accomplishment by week.

3. To serve as liaison with Agape and Fullerton and other appropriate Colleges and Cal State Fullerton to ensure timely performance of all aspects of project contract. Measure: Print out lists of tasks to be accomplished and indicate levels of accomplishment by week.
4. To serve as liaison with Preschool Project Evaluator to ensure that corrections and improvements from all aspects of project contract are made in a timely manner. Measure: Print out lists of tasks to be accomplished and indicate levels of accomplishment by week.
5. To provide training and educational resources which will facilitate the implementation of the Project. Measure: Print out training schedules, lists of allocated educational resources and evaluations of the training sessions.

Job Description for External Evaluator

1. To monitor the implementation Orange County Preschool Plus Evaluation Priorities:
   Use of a Standardized Screening Tool (FirstSTEP);
   Use of a full Child Observation Record kit (High/Scope);
   Use of a Program Evaluation Tool (Early Childhood Environment Rating Scale); and
   Use of Lesson Plans including individualizing and daily notes to make up a comprehensive file for each child.
2. To carry out the following evaluation tasks:
   Assess Project Needs;
   Establish Goals and Performance Objectives;
   Establish An Evaluation Process;
   Select Additional Evaluation Instruments;
   Implement Evaluation Training for Key Staff.
3. To prepare a semi-annual Report describing progress using the following headings:
   Abstract
   The Context of the Evaluation
      a. Description of the evaluation and its rationale
      b. The role of the evaluation and its clients
   The Conceptual Framework of the Evaluation
   The Evaluation Questions
      a. Major questions and sub-questions
      b. Justification of questions
   Research Methods
      a. Measurement instruments and data collection procedures
      b. Research designs

    c. Sampling procedures

    d. Data analysis procedures

    e. Stages of implementation

    f. The process of reporting evaluation findings

    g. Methodological limitations

Findings

    a. Findings regarding each evaluation question

    b. Additional findings

Summary and Conclusions

    a. Summary answers to major evaluation questions

    b. Discussion of significance of findings and their limitations

    c. Conclusions and recommendations

13

Making Decisions about Testing

To understand testing, parents need to understand the political forces that bring it about. A large percentage of each state's budget is allocated to education. The more that is spent on a budget item, the more political it becomes. If we attempt to fool ourselves into believing that education and testing are not highly political, we hurt the educational chances of the children we are responsible for because we will not gather their fair share of resources. Political and business leaders will not support critically needed resources for schools without accountability, which, in the political world, often means testing. Some nations use force to divide up resources. Democratic nations tend to use politics to accomplish this job. This chapter concentrates on creating an understanding of the political concepts that affect school organizations, including influence, control, attitudes and feelings, trust, discontent, and dissatisfaction.

Comprehensive parent involvement treats parents as stakeholders, as described in chapter 3. Parents are involved in key decisions and attend staff meetings. Parents who understand key political concepts make it possible for school staff to think of parents as equals; in turn, parents then feel supported by the staff and administration. This leads quite naturally to sharing key decisions with parents, which makes sense since we now know their support leads to improved student achievement. It is critical that parent leaders understand the concepts in this chapter and that they help other parents participate in decisions as equals with school staff in the areas where staff feel it is appropriate. The decision-making and governance style differs in schools and in school districts. Some groups of teachers prefer a democratic style of school governance, and others a style that is less democratic. My experience suggests that about half of teachers like the former and half the latter approach.

Testing is not the only form of accountability. Here are six additional types:

- Accountability through performance reporting, especially tests that each state gives
- Accountability through monitoring and compliance with standards or regulations, such as individualized education plans (IEPs) for children with disabilities
- Accountability through incentive systems, such as teacher merit pay
- Accountability through reliance on the market, such as vouchers
- Accountability through changing the locus of authority or control of schools, such as community-controlled schools
- Accountability through changing professional roles, as, for example, when teachers review each other for tenure

POLITICAL QUIZ

This quiz offers some basic information and then asks a question. The answers are in the case examples that follow.

1. Authorities make decisions and look at them from a control perspective; influentials seek to influence decisions and look at them from a "lobbying" perspective. Name the authority and the influentials on a recent decision at your school or place of work.

(This case example is from a school district used frequently to answer these questions.)

THE SITUATION: The Adapted Physical Education (APE) Specialists at River Unified School District recently decided to modify the criteria for the admittance of preschoolers into the APE program. Children of this age group and category will henceforth receive guidance from the APE specialists for play therapy activities in specially designed programs for the Special Day Class (SDC) teachers to incorporate into their own programs.

In the past a pull-out approach was used that sometimes offered services to the whole class.

Various pre-K teachers are concerned that their "at risk" population will be overlooked if APE specialists alter their past practice of assessing preschoolers in September and pulling them out in small groups or with the whole class. Meetings have been held involving administrators, teachers, and psychologists to plan, present, and invite response to the redefined preschool assessment philosophy and procedures.

Note: The APE specialists have the primary responsibility for interpreting program philosophy and implementing APE services under the law; therefore, they are "the administrators" for the purposes of this example.

Task 1: The administrator can identify those members of the organization who look at decisions in the organization from an influence perspective. We list four criteria to locate "influence members":

1. Note who, at various staff meetings, have people gathering around them, asking questions.
2. Note who the union leaders are.
3. Identify teacher group leaders through Principal's Cabinet (i.e., a small group of "leader" teachers who have been chosen or who take on the role of bringing information back to the others from the administrator).
4. Note those who have been historically successful in persuading others to their point of view (who have gained credibility with others through their influence in successfully aligning themselves with programs or procedures that have been adopted). They are:
   a. vocal
   b. assertive
   c. have time/experience on the job

Task 2: The administrator can identify those members of the organization who look at decisions in the organization from a control perspective.

The administrators recognize that the APE specialists, the director of special education, and the coordinator of special education are the "controllers" in this situation.

Note: Authorities control those below them in the pecking order; these same authorities become partisans (attempt to influence) when dealing with those above them, or those who control resources they need. List three criteria you can use to locate "control" members."

1. Those who make binding decisions
2. Those who formally evaluate performance
3. Those who are on the administrative flow chart, including the school board
4. Those who "control" by unofficial authority like those with special knowledge or experience with a key issue

Indicate the "control members" in the case and the criteria that apply to them.

Director of Special Education, under criteria #1, #2, #3 in the list right above but not # 4.

Coordinator of Special Education, under #1, #2, #3.

APE Specialists, under #4.

2. Define power as it relates to school goals.

The administrator recognizes that power is the capacity to mobilize resources of the community for the attainment of school goals.

Note: Resources may include: MONEY, PEOPLE, TIME, ENERGY, FACILITIES.

List two indicators that the administration recognized this.

The APE Specialists presented a plan to make "more efficient" use of people utilizing the SDC teachers.

The APE Specialists presented a plan to make better use of teacher/student time thus freeing the APE staff to better service their caseloads, and allowing the student to remain in an integrated, non-fragmented SDC program.

3. When should you "go public" in a political struggle?

The administrator recognizes that private conflicts are taken into the public arena because someone wants to make certain that the power ratio among the private interests most immediately involved shall not prevail. To say it another way, one moves from a behind-the-scenes struggle to open conflict when one sees no other way to win.

The administrators (APE staff) are aware that two of the SDC teachers affected by the program change have tried to mobilize the community (parents) in defense of their past approach.

The Pre-K teachers operated their classrooms with APE services filling (typically) two thirty-minute time slots per week with the APE Specialist administering the effort. The APE. Specialists proposed a new plan that provided more limited Special Education services in a time of decreasing Special Education funds. The Pre-K teachers could mobilize parents to demand additional APE services for their children.

4. Name the faculty from your school who are

   alienated,
   neutral,
   allied with the present administration.

Orientation toward the school may be classified as allegiance when attitudes, feelings, and evaluations are favorable to the school; as apathy or detachment when attitudes, feelings, and evaluations are neutral; and as alienation when attitudes, feelings, and evaluations are negative.

Teacher A: everyone follows/has credibility; is positive about the school.

Teacher B: has perception that he has some influence, but really doesn't. At times he recognizes this and is usually neutral.

Teacher C: eats lunch alone, dislikes administrators, who have been out to get him for years (he thinks); is negative.

5. In a recent decision at your school name the faculty who wanted to influence; put a check by those who felt they could, in fact, influence.

The administrator wants to influence the staff and recognizes that for his/her authority to be effective he/she must have a good deal of freedom to commit resources without the prior consent of the staff.

Example: An administrator, along with a group of math teachers, plans for the expenditure of funds for "math manipulatives" in September. Freedom is needed for the administrator to make various purchases later on for specific items as necessary without having to get a line-item OK on each occasion from the original group. She is successful in the influence attempt and is given the freedom to move ahead without prior consent.

6. Name a principal who has a large bank of good will from her/his faculty and one who does not.

The administrator recognizes that it is possible for the loss of trust to encourage a downward spiral.

The administrators (APE Specialists) in our case realized that continued dedication to program quality in everyone's eyes will help maintain credibility when changes are necessary. All staff were aware that Special Education funds were increasingly being channeled to support "full inclusion" law suits where parents had won the right to place their child in private facilities that offered services not available through public schools. Therefore Special Education had to make reductions in services wherever it was possible.

A principal realizes control/credibility is negatively impacted when loss of trust or confidence occurs. The indicators of declining trust include:

Low morale,

Tension noticed in staff meetings, and

Lack of response in staff meetings.

7. What can the principal with the good will do that the principal lacking good will cannot with respect to negotiating for a new project a school wants at the district office?

The administrator recognizes that successful influence stimulates member support and increased support stimulates more effective influence.

The administrators (APE Specialists) discussed redefining their program with key psychologists and administrators prior to presenting modifications at a general meeting.

Following the announcement of intended APE program modifications at the general meeting, support for the changes was given by the Special Education Administrators when queried by the affected teachers. Realizing the "tide had turned," and that reductions had to be made, most of the teachers eventually accepted the changes positively.

A "positive wave" had been formed.

8. Think of a situation where you have seen a "downward spiral of trust" when a principal caused the staff to lose faith in her/his judgment.

The administrator understands that dissatisfaction begins to be generalized when an undesirable outcome is seen as a member of a class of decisions with similar results. If an administrator takes a stand on a number of issues that ultimately fail, his lack of judgment might be seen as pervasive.

A principal is advised by the district administration that a certain high school would be a good candidate for a year-round program. The principal likes the idea and begins to initiate it. He fails to poll the community, and it resists the concept "en masse." The district office refuses to back him up. He loses credibility. The same principal earlier had banned certain hairstyles on campus, and had been confronted with a large (and publicized) protest. The principal was eventually transferred to a small, remote school.

9. How can successful influence lead to increased staff support?

The administrator recognizes individuals with differing levels of trust in the district/school administration including persons who a) have confidence; b) are neutral; and c) are alienated.

Principal A enters a new school. She requests feedback from each English teacher in the form of a private, one- or two-sentence note asking how he or she feels about a new idea for the English curriculum. She then knows who is amenable to the new idea, who is not, and who may be neutral. She shows the list to her secretary and confirms her idea about which English teachers are most influential, in this case the positive ones. She moves ahead with the curriculum change and it gains general support.

10. How can increased trust lead to greater respect not only in your own school but at other schools? Example?

Authorities control and partisans influence as their primary means of utilizing power.

The administration recognizes that a partisan (influence) group can be said to have exercised influence only if there is a difference in an outcome which can be traced to the group's efforts.

The APE staff realized that gaining approval from the controlling administrators(s) in advance would greatly increase their chances of implementing desired program changes smoothly.

The APE staff researched the need for program modifications in several schools and presented a series of positive reasons for change. Program restructure was accomplished.

11. Think how dissatisfaction, if followed by a series of decisions favoring the same group, can lead to general loss of trust?

The administrator recognizes that a negative influence or backlash may occur when partisans' efforts turn authorities against their preferred outcome. In the present case the top administrators knew they had not granted recent favors to the APE staff.

12. The APE Specialists had received two new computers; in order to maximize their impact, who should get the computers—those with allegiance, the neutrals, or the alienated?

The principal recognizes that there are three ways to influence: constraints can be introduced, inducements offered, or persuasion used. Careful analysis suggests the computers should go to the neutrals. Those with allegiance can be brought along with a few kind words about their children; hence persuasion for them. The negatives will not support the cause even if you give them the computers; hence, use constraints such as loss of parking privileges with them. The neutrals may, however, be tipped into the support column with a computer nudge.

13. We read that authorities should control and partisans should seek to influence as the appropriate use of power. Please explain.

The administrator recognizes the cost of influence, including the sacrifices that a would-be influencer must make in exercising influence and, in particular, the alternative use of his/her resources which he/she forgoes. In this case the Director of Special Education made a judgment that control would not work because the key teachers were not under her authority but were regular classroom teachers. Hence she supported the APE staff in giving the computers to key neutrals, a direct (and successful) influence effort.

14. Sometimes partisans go too far and this can lead to backlash. Example?

Certain parents have expressed disappointment with the loss of the traditional program. These parents have been encouraged to observe the changes and gain assurance, hopefully, that their children are not going to receive less than they should on the next important resource decision.

15. We have seen there are three ways to influence: constraints can be introduced, inducements offered, or persuasion used. Think of a way that the inducement of the computers could have caused a backlash?

The art of influence is often a matter of knowing whom to offer the inducement to. If the neutrals who received the computers were disliked by many teachers, the strategy might well have backfired.

16. Can you offer an example of the "cost of influence"?

Certainly the cost in the case was the hurt feelings of some of the positive teachers who had a hard time understanding why an administrator would give computers to teachers who were neutral rather than to their long time supporters. With patient conversation over time they will no doubt be helped to understand.

17. Often the job of the principal is to "manage discontent" and/or to "contain influence." Can you give an example of each?

In this case a supportive principal was confronted by a group of angry parents who didn't like the decision and demanded that a fence be placed completely around an elementary school or they would go to the School Board. They intuitively knew that even though they had asked for this in the past without success they might win this time. The principal agreed that the fence should have been built completely around from the beginning. She asked the group for help in determining how much additional fencing was needed (giving them some input and control over the situation) and agreed to assist them in going through the appropriate channels. She managed their discontent and contained their influence.

18. What do we mean when we say we "modified the content of the decision" in order to build trust?

A supportive principal, in her hiring of two new teachers, had a disagreement among her staff about whom to select. She modified her decision to favor the teachers who had just lost on the APE decision in order to build trust that she was even handed and played no favorites on the staff.

19. Give an example of a situation where the most discontented staff have the least opportunity to influence a decision.

In this case the discontented parents at campus A have not been influential in the past. On the other hand the chairperson of the parent teacher organization at campus A has been around for years, wielding a great deal of influence. She has a great deal of control as to what direction her organization's resources may take and she was able to swing her school to support the APE decision, even though she was loudly opposed by the discontented parents.

20. What do we mean when we say "offering conciliatory measures in a timely fashion may head off a rebellion"?

There are those who believe that the head of the parent–teacher organization persuaded a friend of hers to propose the fencing of the school mentioned above in order to head off a rebellion of a large group of parents at her school.

21. How could a principal "offer differential access to staff in order to win the support of key neutrals" on an important decision?

At another school the principal readily allowed a group of parents to publish some mathematics curriculum materials and to influence the parents and staff of the school because he knew these parents could help him gain the support of several neutrals from his staff on the APE decision (which he supported).

22. Give an example of the effect of "absorbing new people into the leadership group" as a strategy for heading off an insurrection.

A principal included a neutral teacher on a key committee in order to win the support of other neutrals whose support was needed on a curriculum vote.

23. What do you think of playing off one partisan group against another as a means of stabilizing discontent?

The principal understood that if the teachers who were for and against the new math curriculum were stalled, the neutral teachers would vote for no change and the discontented groups would be quieted, if not pleased.

24. If a group has received more than its share of resources, will it lie back or aggressively seek even more resources? What should you do about their behavior, if anything?

As in other aspects of life, the teachers who have garnered the most favors pursue more favors relentlessly. Give them kind words but no resources.

25. The more liquid a group's resources, the more they will attempt new influence . . . true or false?

Quite true, just as we find it easier to save money if it is not easily available.

26. Confident groups will try to influence decisions constantly—but so will alienated groups. Explain.

These are the teachers who care, on both sides, and they will be busily attempting to achieve their objectives.

27. We have distinguished three means of influence: constraints, inducements, and persuasion. All three are likely to be employed by partisan groups, but any given group will tend to rely on one more

than the other two. For instance, confident groups will rely on persuasion. Examples for neutrals and the alienated?

Neutrals will offer inducements, and the alienated will threaten.

28. How will well-trained principals use the concepts in item 28 in decisions they control with confident, neutral, and alienated groups ?

The confident teachers get affectionate comments, the neutrals the new modems, and the alienated will be isolated.

29. Explain the following four types of school decision making:

Organizational
To use this model you must demonstrate that

    a. Staff objectives are different from Board objectives.
    b. Staff objectives are not the best way to meet Board goals.

The Board wants improved reading scores. An easy test is purchased with the thought that no one on the Board will know the difference.

Rational
The three criteria to use in deciding if this model is in use are:

    a. Board members agreed in writing on certain objectives.
    b. Reference to these objectives was made in the course of decision making.
    c. Outcomes were consistent with objectives.

About the only time we see such rationality in decision making is when there is a severe penalty for not following agreements to the letter, as in a federal or state grant.

Pluralist
Pluralist groups will

1. Concentrate their energies on those issues having the greatest impact on their interests.

2. Develop new alliances as the issues and tactical situations change.
3. Migrate from one political faction to another as political leaders' positions on matters of group concern are modified.

This type of horse trading is typical of people who don't care about the content of a decision but are trying to avoid criticism. They will be owed a vote or two to use in the future.

Ideological
Ideologues will

1. Be very reluctant to compromise, especially on their favorite issues.
2. Push their favorite issue or issues relentlessly.

This type of decision is typical of people with little political experience who were elected on one salient issue like "phonics is the way to teach reading."

14

Parent Involvement Using Shared Decision Making

Comprehensive parent involvement treats parents as stakeholders, as described in chapter 3. Parents are involved in key decisions and attend staff meetings. This leads school staff to thinking of parents as equals, and parents feel supported by the staff and administration. This leads quite naturally to sharing key decisions with parents, which makes sense since we now know their support leads to improved student achievement. Initial aspects of effective decision making, including the choice of a useful decision model that fits the problem at hand, stating the problem accurately and understanding the assumptions behind the problem statement, are all discussed in this chapter.

WHAT IS SHARED DECISION MAKING?

Shared decision making is a process that includes the input of parents, teachers, administrators, community members, and possibly students in decisions about how a school or school district operates. School districts practicing school-based management use this practice. School-based management allows those who are most aware of the educational needs of the local school district to help direct it. In a school-based management system, shared decision making shifts the power from a central authority, such as one individual or a school board, to a broader representation, such as a council or "team." School management becomes a shared responsibility, although the school board is still legally responsible for the decisions made.

Many educators believe that parent representation in key decisions in their child's school is preferable to offering them vouchers and is more likely to lead to an excellent education.

Here are some potential areas of parent involvement in decision making:

After-school activities
Budget issues
Class size
Curriculum/textbook selection
Disciplinary procedures
Length of school day/year
Long-range planning
School lunch programs
Special programs (gifted, remedial, dropout)
Staff evaluation/retention
Student assessment
Training for staff, parents, and community members
Transportation

Parents need to know not only what areas of school life they can be usefully involved in, but how decisions are made in a school that seeks to welcome parent input.

DECISION MAKING DEFINED

Decision making is a process wherein an awareness of a problem, influenced by information, values and beliefs, is reduced to competing alternatives. From these alternatives, a choice is made. The initial aspects of effective decision making include, first, identifying and stating a problem or situation accurately; second, understanding the assumptions behind the problem; and third, choosing a useful decision model to resolve the problem or situation.

Decision making may be defined more specifically in a variety of ways. It can be seen as a problematic state that is reduced to competing alternatives, among which a choice is made based on an estimated outcome. Values affect all decisions that are made. And individuals, depending on their own styles, reach decisions in different ways.

Moralists tend to strive for reaching the "right" decision in the "right" way. *Expedients* tend to want to reach a decision in the method that is the easiest. Then of course there are those who take both seriously and want the right decision reached as quickly as possible.

Individuals tend to fall into four distinct groups when implementing decisions; every school site has staff members who make up these four groups. First are those members who are always willing and able. They never hesitate to volunteer and become involved. They don't ask if they can handle one more job or task—they just do it. They are usually the campus cheerleaders and a pretty energized group of individuals. The second group are those individuals who are willing but not able. These are the ones who need extra help in implementing the decision. The third group are those individuals who are not willing but able. These are the ones who say, "It doesn't concern me" or "I don't need to do it," or else they need an extra incentive to ensure buy-in. These will ask if they will be paid for their after-school hours. Fourth are those individuals who are not willing and not able. With these, it is difficult to bring about the shared decision as they take extra time and instruction by the principal to ensure that the decision will be carried out.

A SEVEN-STEP DECISION-MAKING MODEL

Regardless of how a decision is reached, it may or may not be successfully implemented. Implementation of the decision must be carried out through a plan of action developed with sequential steps to ensure ownership and participation of as many players as possible. A useful decision-making model to facilitate agreed-on decisions contains the following seven basic steps:

1. *Clearly state the problem.* This step sometimes can take the longest, as a deep understanding is paramount to effectively implement a decision-making model. Perhaps the most complex aspect of decision making pertains to the way a decision problem is stated. Sometimes it is appropriate to be very specific; at other times it is necessary to be abstract and general. In this step, you

may need to restate your problem more specifically. It is important that the decision problem be stated in words that are clear to the reader so that accurate assumptions about the problem can be made by all with the information at hand and the way the problem is stated. As a parent, you may have a very specific idea about how you feel the decision should be resolved. Therefore, it is extremely important to state the problem needing to come to a decision based on group reaction. Shared decision making helps assure that the decision will be carried out.

2. *List the assumptions*. Everyone involved with the problem has certain preconceived notions, values, and beliefs. It is important to list all of the assumptions shared by the stakeholders, for without all of the information laid out in advance, the agreed-on decision may not be implemented because so many people disagreed on assumptions and did not realize it.

3. *Decide on the framework*. Decision making takes place in different frameworks or environments. Thus, you have more wiggle room on a decision that affects one school than you do when it affects all schools in the district. In essence, this step establishes the ground rules to which the group will adhere.

4. *List the information sources*. Information must be timely to be useful. It must also be at the right level of detail and presented at the right time. The quality of a decision rests in part on the quality of the information you have available to help make the decision. Reference needs to be given to (1) deciding on who should collect the information; (2) deciding how the information should be gathered; (3) collecting the information; (4) consolidating the information to form a proposal; (5) presenting the proposal using an agreed-on format or process. It is essential that information be presented in a timely fashion to be useful and, likewise, reported at an opportune moment. It must also provide the right elements of detail. The KISS approach works well: "Keep It Short and Simple." Keep to the pertinent and salient facts only.

5. *Decide on values*. By this time in the process, you are now almost ready to make a decision. However, before the final decision can be made, recognition of values must be addressed, for decision making is influenced by the values of those providing data as well as the decision maker's values. In this step, each person involved has very

different perceptions of the same event. Your group needs to be able to recognize the impact value systems have on decision making. For example, a school where most parents are very competitive about the type of college their children will attend may not value full inclusion of special education students as much as a group of parents who are not so focused on college.

6. *List the alternatives.* Decision making is strengthened by having several good alternatives from which to choose in moving to a specific decision choice. To facilitate the process of using alternatives in decision making, it is helpful to state the criteria one uses to judge alternatives and to be aware of the "probability for success" in selecting one alternative over another. You need to be able to recognize the value of stating alternatives in the decision-making process. Better decisions are the result of better alternatives.

7. *Make the decision!* A *consensus* decision-making structure that ensures that all stakeholders have been allowed to speak and express their opinion is important to making a final decision. Another popular approach to making a decision that is used when all factors have equal bearing is a *force-field analysis.* With this strategy, all alternatives and choices toward the final decision are listed. The facilitator then ranks all of the alternatives according to how feasible they will be to solve the problem. Through a forced-ranking process, often the consensus reached can lead to a successful decision.

This seven-step process is effective when dealing with problems that require input from the major stakeholders. However, be aware that not all decisions can or should be accomplished through a shared process. Only your group can determine which decisions should be shared. Past knowledge of the decision-making processes used will help to determine what steps to take and when to use the steps listed in this process.

OTHER DECISION-MAKING PROCESSES

What is the best type of decision-making process? The seven-step model just described provides a generic type of model, but all decision making should start where the staff members or stakeholders are in their development and in each situation. If a school staff is used to being told what to do, a new leader might want to take the easy way and just tell them what needs to be done. With these individuals, the democratic approach might be resisted because previously ideas and input had not been solicited, and the stakeholder may feel unsure about how to follow through without being told how to do something specifically. Of course, in situations where stakeholders are more used to a participative or democratic style, this style should be continued as much as possible. Decisions made democratically do take the most time, but they usually gather greater support from the staff. And this support helps them be more successful than they would be otherwise. While authoritarian decisions are easier to make, they can often have unintended consequences. Teachers and parents may repress their feelings and feel discounted. Tasks will still get done, but the interpersonal problems created may make for new difficulties later on.

Here's a simple checklist of five key steps that can comprise another decision-making model:

1. Identify the major problem.
2. Abstract the salient facts.
3. List possible solutions.
4. List the possible consequences for each possible solution.
5. Decide which solution is the most feasible, justify it, and then carry it out.

No matter which model a school uses, keep in mind that the group process of reaching decisions is only useful when a large group consensus is needed. In other situations, however, a more autocratic approach is most effective: when a decision needs to be made that does not require committed action by the whole group, when a simple decision does not require coordinated effort of many of the group, and when the outcome that will result from the decision doesn't have an impact on staff members.

WHO MAKES THE DECISION?

When it comes to reaching a decision, it is important to know who has the authority to make the decision and who has the responsibility to do so as well. While reaching a decision is important, defining who has the responsibility to make that decision or who has the authority to see it through can have a great impact on how or whether a decision is reached. Sometimes, one may have the authority, but not the responsibility, or just the opposite.

In school and district office administration, the smoothest operations are a result of knowing who is in charge of what and when. The roles of the school board, superintendent, district administration, and school site principal need to be well defined and have clarity on two issues: Whose responsibility is it, and who has the authority? To assist in defining the chain of command, the National School Board Association has developed the following guidelines:

B = Decisions made by the board
S = Decisions made by the superintendent or immediate staff
P = Decisions made by the school site principal
T = Decisions made by teacher or group of stakeholders
A = Decision made by another staff member
C = Decision made by collective bargaining agreement
U = Unclear; clarification is needed before decision is made

Consider your situation and try using these lettered guidelines to answer these questions:

1. Whose decision is it to call off school because of inclement weather?
2. Whose decision is it to change the bus stop from one corner to another?
3. Whose decision is it to change a teacher's grade-level assignment?
4. Whose decision is it to release news to press about honor students?
5. Whose decision is it to determine which textbooks are to be used?
6. Whose decision is it to give teachers a "free period"?

WAYS TO FACILITATE DECISION MAKING

At Iowa Elementary School, where there are many middle-class families, the principal described the school's decision-making approach as follows:

To expand empowerment of school staff and parents we involve as many as possible in different stages of the decision-making process. At our school, each teacher is a member of a school committee representing their grade level. These committees include a Principals' Advisory Committee, a Leadership Committee, a School Improvement/Leadership Committee and the School Site Council. They are also selected to have one individual school wide responsibility. This can range from facilitating weekly staff meetings to handling student leadership activities. This process of shared decision making lets participants know that what they think and how they would like to see something accomplished is important. They are responsible for supporting the essential agreements that are made in that once a decision has been made, whether or not we are for or against it, we agree not to sabotage the decision and will support it and follow through. Our job is to provide different techniques and processes to enable consensus to be reached and to support the staff in decision-making processes. It is also our responsibility to bring to them those things that matter and try our hardest to focus on those things that support our school goals. It is also our responsibility to interfere when necessary to allow teachers and staff to successfully accomplish what they need to get done and not have time taken away from their job of educating students when their decisions aren't necessary.

SITE-BASED DECISION MAKING

Site-based decision making is a strategy occurring in schools throughout the country. To help build a community of professionals sharing unified goals along with individual goals (i.e., teaming, shared decision making, and shared curriculum ideas), a school-based advisory committee or Principal's Advisory Council is helpful. This group of individuals is valuable in providing feedback about how staff members generally feel and what they need in terms of resources and support. It also serves to allow staff members to communicate across grade level lines. While grade-level meetings allow for the potential of consistency, an advisory committee in an open-forum format helps articulation, the sharing of ideas, and the fostering of effective dialogue and communication.

Another reason why shared leadership and site-based decision making is so effective is that creativity and decision-making abilities are widely distributed in the population and not necessarily determined by the position a person holds. A Principal's Advisory Council can help to provide for the effective use of all of these abilities within the formal organization.

While it is the principal's responsibility to establish broad parameters of appropriate behavior, consistent with general school policies and good educational practice, it is also his or her obligation to seek input from individual staff members or identified groups of parents. Allowing wide latitude for problem resolution and final decision making and supporting staff as they share their opinions demonstrates that the principal recognizes that both the private goals of organizational members and the agreed-on school goals affect the school's achievement.

The attainment of a positive-feeling tone comes to a school in many ways, but the crucial foundation for student growth needs the twin pillars of parent and school staff support. It is no surprise that the students with the best overall performance come from loving and responsible homes where what the student learns at school is reinforced. Parents who receive consistent communication from the campus, including notes from the teacher and the principal, demonstrate greater feelings of trust and contentment. Effective organizations are characterized by a variety of communications media and a free flow of information laterally and vertically throughout the organization. Importance must be placed on a variety of communications, including face-to-face and nonverbal cues.

The phrase "A picture is worth a thousand words" applies to schools as well as books. A monthly newsletter sharing what has been happening as well as what lies ahead is important, but these newsy items must be shared in person to ensure that what you say is being understood. Seek first to be understood, then to understand. This is particularly applicable to schools where educators are comfortable using jargon in conversation.

If important information such as a proposed change in curriculum or scheduling will be occurring, then a formal meeting must be scheduled in addition to any written form of communication sent home. Parents knowledgeable about the school's vision are more likely to become involved when they are connected with the school. They are also more likely to be strongly supportive and help spread positive public relations about their school and, hopefully, public schools in general.

At Iowa School, a lively newsletter is sent home at the beginning of each month. This serves to communicate what is happening and what to anticipate during the coming month. A monthly column appears in the PTA newsletter called "Principal Thoughts." This is more philosophical or educationally based and shares educational tips with parents as well as parenting advice. School staff also try to share research or address any parent questions and then link these to the school culture. Staff writes a weekly article in the local newspaper sharing one event from school for that week. Teachers also send home notes attached to weekly or daily homework assignment sheets in addition to a monthly classroom newsletter.

Parents often need to hear things two or three times to be able to truly understand what is happening at school. This is even more true when changes or new learnings are being introduced. As use of the Internet increases in our homes and schools, having a school home page can be a wonderfully effective way to keep communication ongoing. Likewise, through the use of e-mail, two way communication can be encouraged and really being informed can truly occur. This helps build the positive climate and feeling tone desired for your school. With the technology available today, there is little excuse for a lack of communication.

CLEAR, FREQUENT, AND CONCISE COMMUNICATION

Lack of communication and inconsistent implementation of policies are the two key factors that will destroy a positive school climate for staff and parents. Consistency and rationale for why things are occurring as they do are key in building and keeping trust. Clear, frequent, and concise communication is important with parents, as is open communication with staff at all times.

15

Fund-Raising and Writing Proposals

With fewer funds being allocated to education, most schools are looking at creative ways to generate more funds to continue programs and needed staffing. As money is raised by various support groups within the school setting, several issues are raised, including how much, how often, how to determine needs, and how to share control. In this chapter, creative ways of gathering resources are shared together with examples.

In schools where funding for education has been limited, fund-raising for school programs has become a necessity. While the intent for all fund-raising should be to supplement current programs and offerings at schools, in many states fund-raising has become necessary to allow current programs just to exist.

A word of caution must be taken in regard to fund-raising. Communication must be constant about the needs and the purpose for each fund-raising event. The purpose for the event must be directly connected to a school goal, and those involved with the fund-raiser must be in agreement with the decision on how the funds raised will be used.

FUND-RAISING CAN PULL THE SCHOOL COMMUNITY APART

This again is why communication through the entire process is extremely important. If those raising the funds are not in agreement with how the funds will be used, the fund-raiser can pull the school community apart rather than build it up for a common cause. Likewise, a principal can find him- or herself between a rock and hard spot if the Booster Club raises money to build a storage shed for equipment, while the school staff sees the primary need to increase the number of computers for instruction for students.

At Jefferson Elementary, for example, prior to any fund-raising event, a form is completed by the group doing the fund-raising. The form asks that the purpose of the fund-raiser be stated and that it relate to the agreed-on school plan and school goals. It is signed by the principal as well as the PTA president and/or School Site Council to see that the purpose and need are both clearly defined and in support of school goals. Having both PTA and the School Site Council be involved in the process helps ensure accountability and support by all leaders of the school.

ASSESS NEEDS

Jefferson also holds a meeting every spring to assess needs and to develop goals and priorities for the next year. At this meeting, the PTA, the School Site Council, the Booster Club, Friends of Jefferson, and members of the school staff come with a list of needs they have identified. Collectively, they present these ideas, discuss them, and then establish a prioritized list of goals and needs for the next year. From that agreement, they then determine what things can be funded by the school budget and what other funds are needed to enable threatened or proposed programs to become a reality. From that, fund-raisers are set for the next year with the agreement that money raised will fund the first priority first and so on.

Following this process ensures that all of the school community knows exactly what the goals are and what the purpose is of each fund-raiser together with the amount targeted to raise. Jefferson tends to hold about five to six fund-raisers each year. Some are major efforts like gift wrap sales, and others are less demanding, such as cookie dough and frozen pizza sales. Jefferson also works to communicate to parents that the school appreciates their support but realizes that not all fund-raisers will be supported by the entire school community. It requests that they participate in those that are most meaningful to them.

FUND-RAISERS WILL BENEFIT THE
GREATEST NUMBER OF STUDENTS

Jefferson fund-raisers have contributed over $30,000 for the past three years to help continue its high-quality programs and instruction. One other agreement is that fund-raisers will benefit the greatest number of students. For example, Jefferson's Reading Recovery program has trained a teacher to work with students having difficulty learning to read. As a Reading Recovery teacher is only able to work with four students per session for a total of eight per year, parents did not want any school fund-raisers to go toward that program since only a few students benefited from the program. Therefore, the school raises funds for an art lab teacher who teaches all students, and the school budget pays for the training and support of Reading Recovery.

None of the parents in any way were opposed or lacking in support of Reading Recovery, but they wanted the maximum number of students benefiting from the money raised. This is a common goal on which all agree, and this approach allows better buy-in in support of fund-raising events.

WRITING PROPOSALS FOR OUTSIDE FUNDING

Parents with writing skills can help apply for and receive additional funds from government or private sources. Although grant writing is labor-intensive and does not guarantee success, receiving a grant, like childbirth, makes up for a lot of pain. The key to successful grant writing is to first clearly think through the idea, get excited about it, and then describe it clearly in writing.

The second important key to grant writing is to carefully follow the directions given by the funding agency (i.e., clearly respond to each grant section). Typical grant headings include an assessment of need and identification of the target group, identification of project aims, background and significance of the new effort, description of objectives and activities for the project, project design and methods, formative and summative evaluation, plan of operation, budget and cost effectiveness, and commitment and capacity.

Included here are some brief "starter" sentences from proposals to illustrate the various sections. These sections would typically be reordered and renamed to fit the suggestions of the request for proposal from the funding agency. Appendix D is a complete proposal for a dropout and substance abuse prevention program.

Need/Target Population

A winning proposal typically includes a strong presentation of need for the activities that are listed in the proposed project. Take time to gather information from staff and other research sources about the special need for your new effort. This is often a good section to define the target population with lots of descriptive words and numbers to present the need. Try to show how some promising things have been accomplished but that more resources will really make all the difference in building the new approach. Here's one suggestion:

> The magnitude of alcohol and other drug abuse problems has caused increasing nationwide concern among educators, policy makers, and the community at large. Although the rates of drug use may have declined recently, smoking and drinking are still very prevalent teenage activities. In fact, high school students in the U.S. may be more involved with illicit drugs than youth in any other industrialized nation. A recent survey of drug use and dropouts in California and Irvine found . . .

Project Aims

Present the purpose of the project clearly, demonstrating an understanding of what research indicates is effective. For example:

> The aims of the District At-Risk Management Project are to develop a computer management system that will: a) identify potential substance abusers and potential dropouts; and b) use an expert system to connect identified students-at-risk with appropriate interventions which will reduce student risk levels.

Background and Significance

Describe background steps logically leading to current proposal.

Project activities were developed during the past eight years from needs assessments with staff and students and a review of the current literature on high risk and substance-abusing students. Components respond to the research findings, particularly the research on high risk factors for adolescents.

Objectives and Activities of Project

Present a plan for accomplishing the aim of the project, describing the objectives to be accomplished and the activities that will lead to the completion of these objectives.

The proposed program offers a comprehensive holistic approach for preventing alcohol and other drug use by 500 high-risk middle school students. The project addresses the needs of the student, his family, the school, and community, in a comprehensive approach to prevention, through the following:

Student Objective: Decrease the use of alcohol and other drugs in participating students at a .05 level of significance.

Student Activity: Provide individual and small group counseling to identified students.

Assign and monitor progress of identified students in interventions.

School Objective: Increase knowledge and skill levels of educators to implement interventions to reduce risk factors, as measured by pre-/post-assessment.

School Activity: Train staff in use of computer management system to identify and intervene with at-risk students.

Family Objective: Increase parent knowledge of risk and protective factors and improve family management skills, as measured by pre-/post-assessment.

Family Activity: Provide education, support, and referral services for parents of identified high-risk students.

Project Design and Methods

Describe the process of program services as part of the overall design and individual program components more completely, if necessary.

A data-gathering system involving students, parents, school personnel, and community resources to identify students who need help is being developed.

a. A database of all students in the district identifying the lower quadrant based on academics, low test scores, and students exhibiting at-risk behaviors is being developed.
b. A referral form for teachers who have identified a problem with a student and a procedure for handling referrals and tracking disposition of each referral is being developed.
c. An information system to let referring teachers know the disposition of the referral is being developed.
d. A plan for sharing information with parents of students will be developed.

Formative and Summative Evaluation

Describe your evaluation plan, linking it to the measurement of objectives you described. Try to think of an accurate and easily gathered measure of your success in each area. The evaluation ought to focus on two areas:

- Process: Are the steps to achieve outcomes conducive to program success?
- Product: How well is the program accomplishing its specified objectives?

Teacher knowledge and skills in implementing the computer management system will be measured by locally developed pre-/posttests and observation checklists. Outcome evaluation will be based on significant changes (improvement at the .05 level) in baseline data gathered from participant surveys on drug use against which future drug-use and parenting practices of high-risk students' parents will be compared.

Plan of Operation/Budget and Cost-Effectiveness

List general information describing your organization, including the line of authority and role definitions for project staff. Generally describe and support the budget requested.

The Board of Education is responsible for the project and management operations. The project director will coordinate all program activities and supervise project staff.

The budget is adequate to complete project activities and is cost effective in that . . .

Accomplishments/Capacity and Commitment

List any related accomplishments of your program and how they relate to the present effort. Show commitment to continue activities beyond the funding period.

The district has a history of commitment to addressing the needs of at risk students and has developed a number of innovative prevention programs, e.g., STAGES Program, which assists at-risk students in being successful in school despite stressful changes in their lives. This proposal develops an at-risk management system, which complements these existing prevention and identification strategies now in place. This at-risk management system will make a significant impact on reducing student drug use by creating a computerized delivery system for drug abuse prevention and intervention that utilizes the latest research to predict potential abusers and dropouts with an identification system that, in turn, links to some of the most effective interventions in the country. The identification and intervention services will continue after initial funding through . . .

16

Online Parent University Proposal

Presented here is an actual proposal I prepared with a school district to access community resources. Names have been changed to assure confidentiality.

STATEMENT OF NEED

This project grows from needs assessment data gathered in Duncan City School District showing that there is an immediate need for tutoring and other forms of assistance for schools with low State Index scores.

We know from recent research that there is conclusive evidence that in-depth parent involvement in classrooms leads to improved school performance of their children.[1] It is further important to know that if parents are themselves involved in improving their skills, they will be more likely to understand the need to support their children by helping do homework.

We propose to focus not only on parent involvement in classrooms but on parent instruction of children in their home. To accomplish this we plan to operate the Online Parent University, which will have two goals. First, [we hope] to train parents to help their children to learn critical skills at home. Second, we believe that parents need to become employed and to advance beyond minimum wage jobs in the local economy. The Online Parent University seeks to provide the education and job training to make this possible through collaboration with the organizations listed above.

We further propose additional services for our children prior to kindergarten with a focus on the help of parents, with foundation funding. In order to motivate parents to seek a GED and other appropriate training we believe a Career Ladder system should be established so that parents can see a clear path to increased income for their families. This will require the participation of key entry level employers such as schools, hospitals, county and city human service agencies, fast food restaurants, hotels and motels, banks and dozens of others. Employers' Training Resource could help parents from the Online Parent University who are ready for entry level employment. The arrangements need to indicate that parents will receive tutoring and mentoring to (1) become employed; (2) stay employed; (3) move up above minimum wage levels of responsibility.

EXPERIENCE IN PROVIDING SIMILAR SERVICES

Duncan City School District has experience operating prekindergartens through its Child and Family Development Office. We operate Even Start and the Parent University with locations at East Hills Mall, Mercado Latino, and McKinley Elementary Schools. We are especially pleased to have the support of Duncan Adult Education, the Nursing and Early Childhood Programs at Duncan College, and the Child Development and Nursing Programs at Cal State–Duncan to make this program possible.

We will provide new services (we are careful in this project not to budget for services which exist at present) in the areas of anti-tobacco training, family planning, prenatal care, parent (health) education, pediatric care, and early intervention services (focusing on disabilities).

This project focuses on other areas of services as well, including mental health, nutrition, dental, vision services with differing levels of training to provide support to low-income children and families. We see nursing students being utilized to (1) deliver health instruction, (2) provide prevention training and (3) gather data and carry out program evaluations.

MISSION STATEMENT

We will train parents to help their children to learn critical skills at home using a combination of our present instructional delivery systems in the existing Parent University and the new Online Parent University.

Second, we believe that parents themselves need to become employed and to advance beyond minimum wage jobs in the local economy. We will offer Job Training for Parents. Each of our four locations will begin offering Mentoring and Employment Training to the parents of the participating children. These services will be offered at first on a noncredit basis and later for credit. Students would initially complete their high school equivalency diploma and then begin work on their associate of arts degree. We will place them in an appropriate level of employment at the earliest opportunity.

We will help parents learn to develop prereading and oral language instructional skills as they assist their children to use an increasingly complex and varied vocabulary. We will seek to help parents guide their children as they develop and demonstrate an appreciation of books and, in the case of non-English background children, progress toward acquisition of the English language.

Related to this effort is our plan to create an education and health data base of participating children and their parents. This in turn will become part of the Online Parent University Profiles, which will be updated two times a year.

OBJECTIVES OF THE ONLINE PARENT UNIVERSITY

Parents will help staff to implement:

Screening and Assessment
Use of a Standardized Screening Tool for preschool children;
Use of a full Child Observation Record kit; and,
Implementation of Lesson Plans including individualizing of instruction and daily notes to make up a comprehensive file.

Also:

Daily monitoring of each center and classroom using a Health and Safety checklist; and,
Evaluation of each classroom and play environment using, as appropriate, the following procedures:

- Children will be screened using the FirstSTEP Screening Test for Evaluating Preschoolers for Ages 2.5 to 6, which uses such tasks as picture completion, visual position in space, problem solving and auditory discrimination to determine skill levels in the following areas: Cognitive, Language, Motor, Social-Emotional, Adaptive Behavior, and Parent–Teacher Communication.

• This would be followed by the High Scope Child Observation Record for Ages 2.5 to 6 years and, later, the Early Childhood Environment Rating Scale, a program evaluation tool. Categories for these instruments are seen under the Program Evaluation section later in the proposal. These are proven instruments and have been used for years with Head Start children throughout the country.

HEALTH PROFILES

Many of the families that will participate in this project have unmet health needs, especially dental problems. The Profiles will contain information about each parent and her/his family's progress in dental care, anti-tobacco training, family planning, prenatal care, parent education, child care, pediatric care, early childhood education services, and early intervention services (focusing on disabilities). These Profiles will be updated at the beginning and end of each school year in Phase 1 of the project. More frequent updates may occur later in the Project.

Education Profiles

Develop phonemic, print and numeracy awareness;
Understand and use oral language to communicate for different purposes;
Understand and use increasingly complex and varied vocabulary;
Develop and demonstrate an appreciation of books; and,
In the case of non-English background children, progress toward acquisition of the English language.

We will create the Online Parent University Mentoring Program. It will assist Parent University Parents at our four Centers to prepare for, obtain and maintain successful employment and further education through job and personal development mentoring. Mentoring will be carried out by work-study students from colleges that will help existing and new entry level employees move toward living wage positions.

With respect to employment we will help parents:

Obtain a high school equivalency diploma
Obtain entry level employment
Increase training and experience
Retain employment

The Online Parent University will work with participating institutions to see that a variety of faculty and students are recruited to provide the services listed above. A key concept will be "training of trainers" where more skilled individuals train those who are learning new skills and understandings.

Parent education is enhanced by adding options that lead to a career path, including opportunity to improve their English language skills, if needed, and to complete a high school equivalency program. We will work to develop cohorts of parents who can support each other in these classes. We will also create a Mentoring & Employment Program to provide group and individual help to these parents. The courses will be offered by the participating educational institutions.

ADULT EDUCATION AND COMMUNITY COLLEGE INVOLVEMENT WITH THE ONLINE PARENT UNIVERSITY

Overview

It is proposed that an online program be developed to offer training through Duncan Adult Education and Duncan College programs for Online Parent University parents. This program would build online aspects into the many existing courses listed on pp. 126ff. The cost of online development would be covered in part by the Average Daily Attendance funding available for courses that qualify for listing with Duncan Adult Education and Duncan College. This would be done at the Centers where parents would have internet access. Courses leading to a high school equivalency diploma or test of General Educational Development (GED) will be offered. Instruction in parenting would be offered by non-credit programs and health and early childhood classes would be offered by credit programs through Duncan College. Additional classes in areas where entry level jobs are available would be offered. Courses would typically include both classroom and on-line segments for beginning students. More experienced students may elect to use online-only courses already available and others as they are developed.

Courses at Cal State Duncan would be at both the undergraduate and graduate levels and would serve parents who qualify to take them as well as teachers and other school staff who wish to learn more about effective parent involvement in schools. Some of these courses are now available online, some have online aspects and others can be developed with online or online segments.

Courses in parent education and parent involvement can be developed, both from segments of existing courses and from materials available in Appendix A.

Proposal

NONCREDIT ELEMENT: Noncredit programs through Duncan Adult Education will be offered. They will present a program for Online Parent University parents leading to a GED and/or offer parenting classes. English classes would also be included. These classes will be bilingual as needed. Existing courses are as follows:

The Duncan City School District Parent University is offering eight parenting programs this fall. . . . In addition, the Family Literacy Program is offering ESL, GED, Citizenship Preparation, and Computer Classes.

Active Parenting: A Six-Week Video-Based Program in English and Spanish

This state-of-the-art, video-based program has already benefited millions of families in the United States. Parents are provided with skills that will help them develop cooperation, responsibility, courage and self-esteem in their children. This program is most appropriate for parents of two- through twelve-year-olds.

Active Parenting of Teens: A Six-Week Video-Based Program in English and Spanish

This program is geared to help parents prepare their teens and preteens for the challenges of early adulthood. Parents will learn how to gain cooperation from your teenager and avoid common teen conflicts. Each session also includes valuable information on how to address critical issues such as drug and alcohol use, teen sexuality, and violence.

Confident Parenting: A Ten-Week Program in English

The social learning approach is used in this theory-based program. Parents will learn how to create a positive atmosphere in their homes. It also teaches effective limit-setting procedures so parents will not feel victimized by their children's misbehaviors. Parents will learn the skills of effective praising, effective ignoring, mild social punishment, "time-out" procedures for misbehavior, and how to set up special incentive systems.

Confident Parenting II—The Reunification Program: A Ten-Week Program in English and Spanish

This program is designated for parents who are required to take parenting classes. It follows the regular Confident Parenting Program in addition to required components that satisfy the Reunification Program criteria.

Developing Capable People: A Ten-Week Program in English and Spanish

This program is designed for parents and school staff members. It teaches effective strategies and techniques to help reduce family conflicts, promote better family management, encourage children to be responsible for their actions, develop strong beliefs in personal capability, and communicate more effectively.

Los Niños Bien Educados: A Twelve-Week Program in English and Spanish

This program is designed specifically for parents who are Spanish-speaking and parents of Hispanic origin. It teaches a series of child management skills within a value system that is particularly Hispanic—raising children to be "bien educados." Traditional role, gender, and age expectations, types of cultural adjustments, and other issues pertinent to Hispanic parenting in the United States are covered.

Effective Black Parenting: A Twelve-Week Program in English

This culturally sensitive program was developed specifically for African American parents. It teaches an achievement orientation to African American parenting, including the "Path to the Pyramid of Success for Black Children," special coverage of such issues as Pride in Blackness, and specific child management and communication skills.

MegaSkills: A Ten-Week Program in English and Spanish

MegaSkills have been called the "inner engines of learning." They are qualities, skills, and attitudes needed for success. This program is designed to help parents help their children succeed in school and beyond by helping them learn the basic values, attitudes, and behaviors that determine success.

Beginning ESL

This course is for students who cannot read or write in either their native language or in English. It is also for students who are literate in their native language, but speak little or no English. The course is designed for students who have limited abilities to communicate their needs by using simple phrases and sentences.

Intermediate ESL

This course is designed to strengthen communication skills for work or social settings, and to enable students to comfortably participate in community activities. It is also designed to teach students to follow written directions, comprehend conversations containing unfamiliar vocabulary, participate in face-to-face conversations, and make themselves understood.

Computer Introduction

The most popular class for beginning computer users. We start from "This is the ON button" and build up from there. Using the popular software program Microsoft Works 4.0, this course provides a student with those basic skills to operate their own computers, as well as preparing them for more advanced studies.

Computer MS Word Internet

This class in the MS OFFICE sequence is state-of-the-art word-processing. Excellent preparation for other software in the MS OFFICE sequence such as MS EXCEL, MS POWERPOINT, and MS ACCESS. Also, learn how to explore the World Wide Web. Find information and products from all over the world. You will learn how to connect to the internet, how to send and receive e-mail from your friends. Surfing cyberspace should be no more difficult than changing the channels on your TV. Recommend "Computer Introduction" be taken as a preparatory course.

Citizenship Preparation

If you have been a legal resident for five years or more, you may be eligible to apply for U.S. Citizenship. The Citizenship Preparation course will assist students in completing the citizenship application (N400 form) and in preparing for the written examination (the Basic Citizenship Skills Examination) and oral interview with I.N.S. You must attend an orientation meeting before beginning the class.

GED Classes

Must be eighteen years or older to enroll in this class. Reading, writing, math, history, and science are the five subjects covered in this class to prepare you for the GED test. Passing the GED is an equivalent to a high school diploma. Taking the GED class is also suggested for those students who need fifty or more credits to earn a diploma.

CREDIT ELEMENT: Duncan College will offer instruction in appropriate health care, early childhood education, and other areas where employment is possible.

ENROLLMENT ASSUMPTIONS: It is assumed that the three Centers will enroll approximately seventy-five parents in the pilot program. They would probably take either basic education and/or health and childhood classes. In addition, a Mentoring & Employment Program for all Online Parent University parents will serve parents in class size cohorts of twenty-five and could eventually serve hundreds of parents as mentors are found.

It is estimated that about half of these parents would be interested in the GED program. About two-thirds of these parents would need English classes. It is assumed all parents would enroll in parenting and child development classes. Duncan College could offer course work in basic health care with special emphasis against the use of alcohol, drugs and tobacco. It would also offer work in Early Childhood Education.

FINANCES: While the Online Parent University Proposal Grant will cover administrative salaries and supplies, teachers' salaries would be paid for by the College and financed by claiming ADA reimbursements. This is more advantageous to the College than direct payment for courses from the grant.

COMMUNITY AND PARENT INVOLVEMENT

The Online Parent University will have an Advisory Committee which will provide input from the community and parents to guide the Project. . . . In order to be sensitive to community cultural diversity and the needs of the various populations served by the Center, a variety ethnic and income groups are represented.

PROGRAM EVALUATION

Children will be screened using the FirstSTEP Screening Test for Evaluating Preschoolers, which uses such tasks as picture completion, visual position in space, problem solving and auditory discrimination to determine whether the child might have a disability. This would be followed by the High Scope Child Observation Record for Ages 2.5 to 6 years and, later, the Early Childhood Environment Rating Scale, a program evaluation tool. We would also use Performance Indicators such as those seen below.

Evaluation Objectives

Use of a Standardized Screening Tool;
Use of a full Child Observation Record kit; and
Lesson Plans including individualizing and daily notes to make up a comprehensive file.

Also:

Daily monitoring of each center and classroom using a Health and Safety checklist; and
Evaluation of each classroom and outdoor play environment using the Early Childhood Environment Rating Scale.

Also:

Develop phonemic, print, and numeracy awareness;
Understand and use oral language to communicate for different purposes;
Understand and use increasingly complex and varied vocabulary;
Develop and demonstrate an appreciation of books; and
In the case of non-English-background children, progress toward acquisition of the English language.

In addition to the preceding items, educational performance measures have been established to ensure that children:

Know that letters of the alphabet are a special category of visual graphics that can be individually named;
Recognize a word as a unit of print;
Identify at least ten letters of the alphabet; and
Associate sounds with written words.

Health Objectives

Assess to insure the following have been carried out:

Administration of immunization requirements for preschool entry;
Administration of inhaled medication.

Provide information about the following:

Substance abuse reduction (ATOD);
Healthy/safe environments;
Availability of health/nutrition education.

Also, reduce preventable causes of:

Death/infant mortality/injury;
Disability/chronic illness;
Child abuse/neglect; domestic violence.

Parent participants will be assessed to see to what extent English language competence, level of education, and job experience affect the levels of support needed to be successful in (1) life skills, (2) self-advocacy, (3) gaining employment, (4) retaining employment once achieved, and (5) moving to additional training and higher level income.

Evaluation will be an important function and an integral part of program implementation both on the formal and informal levels. The results-based model will consist of the following ongoing steps:

Clarify the intent of the evaluation program as required.
Design data procedures based on measurable outcomes.
Collect data.
Summarize, analyze data.
Determine program results.
Report data to specified audiences.
Review and modify.

Evaluation Procedures

The evaluation of all children in participating programs utilizes clear standards and focuses upon both process (are the steps taken to achieve outcomes conducive to program success?) and product (how well is the program accomplishing its specified objectives?). Because the evaluation is designed to be cyclical, so as to provide continuous feedback to the program, it will provide a formative evaluation process.

NOTE

1. Anne T. Henderson, and Nancy Berla, *A New Generation of Evidence: The Family Is Critical to Student Achievement*, ED 375 968 (Columbia, Md.: National Committee for Citizens in Education, 1994).

17

Lessons from Large-Scale Parent Involvement Efforts

This chapter describes three nationwide programs where parent involvement has been critical in providing support to students as they work to improve their school performance.

HEAD START SUPPLEMENTARY TRAINING PROGRAMS IN PROVIDING CHILD DEVELOPMENT ASSOCIATE/COMPETENCY-BASED TRAINING[1]

In 1965, Head Start was in its second year, and the talk of the education community focused on how powerful Head Start parents were in determining the daily operation of many Head Starts. They differed from state to state and city to city, but almost everywhere, parents were responsible for who got hired as staff members, who got to be board and advisory committee members in charge of policy, and how budget funds were allocated. At that time, Head Start was under attack from many groups that objected to the dominant role being played by parents, not the least of whom were teacher organizations and other school groups.

I was involved in an effort to delay publication of cover articles by three national weekly news magazines that were all written to expose the poor attendance of Head Start aides, most of whom were parents, at required training activities. We negotiated ninety days to improve the training program and were able to do it by making two changes. First, we said that aides could decide where they wanted to go for training, either to a site in their local area, such as their Head Start Center, or to the university in their area where they had been assigned to attend. They universally chose their own centers. The child development professors were not willing to teach in the poverty locations of the centers, but their doctoral candidates most often were. These folks became the new leaders, and the parents gave them excellent support.

The second change was aimed at improving classroom instruction. The aides were asked to choose a colleague who always raised her hand when she didn't understand the teacher's statements. This aide was designated the class assistant and received a small fee for her (there were very few male aides) service.

These two policy changes recognized the important role of aides (parents), and Head Start has had strong parent leadership ever since. The training was named the Head Start Supplementary Training/Child Development Associate (HSST/CDA) program. The training programs are intended to prepare Head Start classroom aides, to meet the competency requirements of the CDA credential.

THE URBAN/RURAL SCHOOL DEVELOPMENT PROGRAM: AN EXAMINATION OF A FEDERAL MODEL FOR ACHIEVING PARITY BETWEEN SCHOOLS AND COMMUNITIES[2]

In 1970, the U.S. Office of Education, through the Bureau of Educational Personnel Development, initiated a program promoting community–school collaboration, which was called the Urban/Rural School Development Program. Designed to train educational personnel, primarily experienced teachers, at schools in low-income communities characterized by student underachievement, it included twenty-six sites. The purpose of this effort was to demonstrate that federal funds could strengthen the educational resources of the total school community through a joint effort between the school staff and the community. The program operating in Hardwick, Vermont, for example, uncovered a typical practice in high school operations that was changed once parents were given the majority vote on the council that governed the project.

Most high school principals in 1970 were given a common budget for both varsity sports and intramural activities. Varsity sports then received virtually all of the funding, and few complaints ever reached the school boards across the land. Under the Urban/Rural Council in Hardwick, the parents decided to apportion the funds equally between the two programs. This led to major conflict, and the council won. This project had decided to include the most powerful people in the community, such as the editor of the newspaper, the leading attorney, and the chief of police on the council, and they often sided with the parents.

It was concluded that parity in community involvement between the school and its community is a viable and effective possibility. The installation of urban/rural programs did restructure the relationship between the community and the school. The participation of community members had a definite effect on the nature of the training programs developed locally. The School/Community Council has become a workable administrative unit. This program allowed community members, especially parents, to have a channel to develop community education and participation.

NATIONAL DROPOUT PREVENTION CENTER AT CLEMSON UNIVERSITY, CLEMSON, SOUTH CAROLINA

This center came about when a meeting of individuals from each state who were responsible for dropout prevention were asked to attend a meeting in Washington, D.C. They realized that they would benefit if they could meet from time to time, and a small group of them began to look for a source of funding. The source found was a large soft-drink firm, and the key players were the board chairman and his wife, who had been a high school dropout. She became the inspiration for the development of an annual conference and later the center at Clemson University.

From the very beginning, school staff responsible for dropout and substance abuse prevention have recognized the critically important role parents can play in prevention activities:[3]

> This manuscript analyzes the impact of parental involvement on dropout prevention. It includes a review of the literature and a research project which indicates that a positive correlation does exist. The research project focused on a small sample of tenth grade at-risk students and compared them to a random sample of tenth grade students whose parents were members of the PTA. The author concludes that parental involvement addresses

important school wide issues such as student achievement and dropout prevention efforts. Specifically, parent involvement programs: provide promising possibilities for effective school research; produce innovative approaches to problem solving; promote partnership between school and community; and present new challenges to the leadership and the management of schools.

PARENTING HELP/SUPPORT

Here are some tips for attaining parent involvement, derived from the work described earlier:

Reach out actively to involve parents whose support is critical for improving the life chances of their children.

Provide individual, group, and family therapy for youth and families.

Offer parents help through parenting and other skill-building courses, support groups, and aid in accessing social services.

Provide pregnant teenagers with prenatal and postnatal care, education about the effects of drugs on unborn babies, and treatment to help them stop their substance use.

Offer day-care services for parents of preschool children.[4]

"HOW DO THESE PROGRAMS RELATE TO ME, THE READER?"

It is a long way from a parent involvement program at a single school or educational agency to a national program involving thousands of people. But each one of these national programs started at a single site, and many approaches were tried and evaluated before we found a plan that could work in many locations. And even then political factors had a great influence. Any time you are involved in setting up a new way to accomplish an educational task, you bump into people who have been doing the task another way. These people have to be convinced that your idea will provide better results with no more effort than the present approach.

NOTES

1. Ann Gilman and Diane Signatur, *An Assessment of Head Start Supplementary Training Programs in Providing Child Development Associate Competency Based Training. Vol. IV: Case Studies of Eight HSST/CDA Training Programs,* ERIC ED 164 140 (1978).

2. James V. Terry and Robert D. Hess, *The Urban/Rural School Development Program: An Examination of a Federal Model for Achieving Parity between Schools and Communities,* ERIC NO: ED 126 022 (1975).

3. Saul Hinden, *How Does Parent Involvement Affect Student Achievement and Dropout Prevention Efforts?* (Clemson, S.C.: National Dropout Prevention Center, 1989).

4. William Callison, *Dropout Prevention Handbook: Apprenticeships and Other Solutions* (Lancaster, Pa.: Technomic, 1994).

18

A California Community Comes Together Working to Solve the Problem of Illiteracy

Bernard J. Herman and Geri Marshall Mohler

This chapter is about a California community (Bakersfield in Kern County) that has approached educational problems in a collaborative and unified way. Businesses, educators, and service organization representatives discovered solutions in the most unexpected places.

Kern County, California, is not your typical county; it is not even your typical California county. Equal in size to Massachusetts, it is the home of *The Grapes of Wrath*, Cesar Chavez, Edwards Air Force Base, and Buck Owens; a land of snow-covered mountains and blazing hot deserts, teeming with oilfields, and the most productive farmland in the world. Bakersfield, the county seat, is five hours from San Diego, San Francisco, Las Vegas, and Reno; two hours from the country's highest mountains, prettiest beaches, and Los Angeles. Kern County sounds like a place with plenty of opportunities and potential. Within the boundaries of this Central Valley area, however, are startling realities. The following statistics demonstrate pointedly why Kern County residents have taken on the task of trying to improve their community through a unique collaborative effort of businesses, education, and social service agencies.

DEMOGRAPHICS

Kern County has grown at a rate faster than California overall. California grew 13.8 percent between the 1990 and 2000 census. By comparison, Kern's population grew by 21.4 percent.

Thirty-two percent of the population is children ages zero to seventeen, with 38.4 percent of those children being of Hispanic or Latino ethnicity. In addition, 16.7 percent of all families speak English less than "very well," and 31.1 percent of families are headed by a single mom or single dad. Thirty percent of all families with children under five are living in poverty. Of the 58,213 impoverished children in Kern, 65 percent were Hispanic/Latino, and 36 percent were under age six.

Kern County is among the poorest fifteen metropolitan regions in the nation and the poorest twelve counties in the state. Its annual average unemployment rate was 11.8 percent compared to the rest of California, which averages 6.7 percent, with unemployment in seven Kern communities as high as 20 and 30 percent. Many Kern County residents are in agricultural work with an average wage of only $16,220, about half of the 2000 average annual wage of $35,550.

Since 1991, Kern's student population has grown by 20 percent. Nine percent of the student population age six to seventeen are provided special education services, with more than half of this number having specific learning disabilities, typically in reading.

Forty non-English languages are spoken by Kern County students, with 21 percent of the total student population considered English learners (formerly ESL).

Although high school dropout rates fell dramatically over the past decade, from 7.2 percent to 2.8 percent, Kern still ranks forty-first of the fifty-eight counties in California.[1]

The greater Bakersfield area is the county seat for Kern County. It encompasses about 60 percent of the total population of the county. With the aforementioned statistics as a stimulus and catapult, a problem-solving mind-set was created, and the Greater Bakersfield Vision 2020 came into being.

THE GREATER BAKERSFIELD VISION 2020

This vision was the result of an effort initiated in 1998 that eventually involved thousands of residents of the Bakersfield, California, community, including youth, over four hundred volunteers, and tens of thousands of volunteer hours on the part of some outstanding, dedicated individuals in designing and implementing a process to develop an actionable plan for the community's future.

Vision 2020 was an open, inclusive, highly participative four-phase process that was an outgrowth of several previous attempts to develop a strategic plan for the community's future. Through community-wide meetings, small-group meetings, and high school meetings, residents assessed community strengths and weaknesses, and then they participated in envisioning the future. Strategies were developed by focused teams, which resulted in an Action Plan, or "blueprint," for the community's future. That Action Plan was handed back to the community in January 2001.

While much has been accomplished in the first few years of this twenty-year plan, there is much more to do. Many of the initial implementation time frames recommended by the teams building the action plan were very aggressive. This is typical of organizations going through strategic planning for the first time. There is a high level of energy, enthusiasm, and a bias for action. While some of the time frames have not been met, in most cases there is considerable forward motion.

What has been truly inspiring is that the level of collaboration in the community has grown even stronger. For example, city and county governmental bodies and agencies collaborating; educational institutions collaborating across district boundaries and across institutional barriers; and business and community-based organizations working together to solve problems. More than 100 agencies and organizations are actively involved in implementing the community's plan, and more than 150 Vision Force volunteers from across the community continue to monitor and urge implementation of the Action Plans.

A Vision 2020 "mind-set" continues to grow—one that emphasizes collaboration: "no one needs to get the credit, let's just get it done"; and learning from each other: "we don't need to duplicate efforts in a scarce resource environment, let's collaborate on the best way to accomplish the goal and move forward."

The city of Bakersfield adopted the Vision 2020 Action Plan and incorporated many of the strategies into its own action plans, including the goal setting of the City Council. Kern County also adopted the Action Plan and has monitored its own progress in accomplishing those strategies and actions specific to its governmental responsibilities.

The various educational institutions—including the Kern County Superintendent of Schools, Kern High School District, Bakersfield College, and California State University–Bakersfield—have embraced the community's vision and have attempted to implement the vision in the ways they can best participate—through collaboration and individual actions. The Greater Bakersfield Chamber of Commerce, Downtown Business Association, and other organizations have also incorporated the community's plans into their own programs of work. Some results to date include the following:

- The "Connecting Kern County" project, a joint County of Kern Administrative Office and City of Bakersfield Economic Development Department, brought hundreds of residents to the table to assess telecommunications and other infrastructure needs to accommodate the new economy future.
- Recognition of the difficulties of children exiting the foster care system provided the impetus for the formation of the Kern Youth to Adult Project.
- Many of the community planning strategies and actions have been incorporated in the recommendations for update of the 2010 General Plan.
- The city and county came to agreement on the transportation alternative that can move the community toward solving its transportation infrastructure problems.
- KernLearn, developed by the Kern High School District as an online assessment tool and help for students, went live in October 2001. Its training, assessment, and tracking programs have been provided to other school districts in an effort to achieve a seamless transition between grade levels.
- A Youth Leadership Bakersfield program was identified in the visioning process as a need and is now in its third year. This program involves up to three students from each public and private high school who exhibit the potential for leadership. These are not the student body officers. The students spend six days during the year learning from the leaders in such areas as energy, business, agriculture, the arts, law enforcement, and education.
- The city followed through with its plans to hire an urban forester to help protect and expand the tree canopy, identified by the Kern Tree

Foundation as a great way to clean the air as well as provide shade and be esthetically pleasing. The city adopted revised landscape standards for new commercial developments as a first step in raising landscaping standards.

- Community policing was identified as an important step for a safer community, and the Bakersfield Police Department and Kern County Sheriff's Office have developed substations in selected neighborhoods.

- The city of Bakersfield staged a charrette process in May 2001, in which residents were invited to share their ideas for an improved Heart of the City where people would want to live, work, and play. Many of those concepts are moving forward by the Downtown Vision Force, including streetscapes, the development of seventy-four urban-style cottage homes, a $21 million, 180-unit senior housing project, an "Arts District," a downtown Aqua Center, and a community ice rink.

Bakersfield's image was a major element of the vision that came back from the community. Vision 2020 took the lead in pulling together an Image Vision Force to hire a research firm for the purpose of first identifying the city's image in the "outside world" and how it got that way, in order to build an image and marketing campaign for the community. Throughout the Vision 2020 process, residents and business leaders alike recognized the importance of improving the image of Bakersfield and the impact that could have on its future.

When the Action Plan was handed back to the community for implementation, the official role of the organization was complete. However, it became apparent that in order for the Action Plan not to just end up on bookshelves, it was important to maintain an organization whose role it would be to do some follow-up: prioritize actions when necessary, review the suggested lead organizations, close the gaps, continue to look for synergies across jurisdictional and functional lines, update the community on progress, and keep the momentum going and be a catalyst for action. Thus, Vision Forces in the areas of Community Planning and Transportation, Downtown, Economic Development, Education and Life Long Learning, Image, Quality of Life, and Youth and Family were created. A complete Vision 2020 update can be seen at www.bakersfieldvision2020.com.

TARGET READING FIRST

The Education Vision Force developed thirteen strategies. One of those strategies, "Target Reading First," was selected as being the highest priority. The Vision Force recognized that reading is the number one factor in determining a student's ability to be successful in any other course of study. No one can argue that reading is the critical building block to success in school and as an adult. At the same time, the road to proficiency is a struggle for many children. More than thirty-four thousand children come to school from homes where English is not the primary language. Others come from environments where reading is not commonplace or encouraged.

No matter what their background or circumstance, the challenge must be to help these children not just become readers but also comprehend and develop sound reasoning skills. Research shows that if students have not mastered reading skills early in their school career, they have an increasingly difficult time catching up with their classmates. Too often this situation leads to frustration and increases the risk of academic failure. We know that society will pay an extremely high price if an inability to read prevents these children from growing into productive citizens.

When asked, "What is reading?" a kindergarten boy replied, "It's like telling a story in your head." Reading is a lot more than that; it is a communication tool and a complex skill that involves the coordination of phonetic, graphic, syntactic, semantic, and pragmatic information. Reading is the first skill children must have in order to learn other subjects.

Children who are introduced to reading at an early age and are supported in this skill in the home, in school, and in the community are more successful students and adults.

Literacy is more than reading; it is an individual's ability to read, write, and speak, compute, and solve problems at levels of proficiency necessary to function on the job, in the family of the individual, and in society. There is a strong correlation between educational achievement and employment and the economy. Jobs of the future will require increasing levels of education. Strong educational performance is required for our community to attract and retain high-paying jobs.

The problem in Kern County is obvious, given these additional statistics:

Fifty-nine percent of Kern County third graders and 40 percent of sixth graders scored at/below the fiftieth national percentile ranking in reading.

Thirty-two percent of students failed the high school exit exam in English; 61 percent failed math.

In 2002, 56 percent of California State University, Bakersfield (CSUB) freshmen needed remedial English; 55 percent needed remedial math.

Seventy-five percent of unemployed adults have reading or writing difficulties.

Twenty-eight percent of children in Kern County live in poverty (over fifty-eight thousand).

The overall goal of Target Reading First was established as "Read by 9 & 9." That is, by the year 2020, 90 percent of children age nine in Greater Bakersfield will be proficient or better in reading skills, and 90 percent of ninth-grade students will be proficient or better in mastering reading content. To implement a plan to achieve this goal, a collaborative structure representing education, business, and the community was created in October 2002.

A *collaborative* is defined as "A multiagency group that has full knowledge and shared responsibility for outcomes." Its role is to

assess what needs to be done,
convene the experts,
identify best practices,
inventory what is currently being done,
identify the gaps,
set the strategy/action to achieve goals,
determine the outcome measures,
implement the strategies;
identify resource needs and available resources, and
monitor progress.

At the first meeting of the Target Reading First Collaborative, consisting of more than one hundred members, the group determined factors that influence low reading scores. The group identified fifty-five key factors, with lack of parental involvement as the most significant of these factors followed by school readiness, the value placed on education/literacy, and poverty.

We want children to learn to read so they can read to learn in later years. Specifically, by age 9 a student should be able to do the following:

- Read grade-level materials independently.
- Develop spelling patterns, roots, and affixes.
- Use conventions of spelling and print paragraphs; end sentence punctuation.
- Clarify new words; summarize reading.
- Answer questions that require analysis, synthesis, and evaluation of grade-level text.
- Support answers to questions.

By ninth grade, a student should have these skills:

- Apply knowledge of word origins to determine meaning of new words.
- Read and understand grade-level material.
- Make progress on reading two million words annually.
- Read and respond to historically or culturally significant works of literature.
- Conduct in-depth analyses of recurrent themes.

A mission statement was also developed, which reads:

The "Target Reading First" Collaborative will create a culture of reading by coordinating efforts that focus results in increasing exposure to and practice of reading by our children and by providing leadership to achieve the Vision. This will be accomplished through:

Identifying and evaluating community resources and gaps;
Linking people, programs and organizations;
Identifying and supporting necessary resources, including funding, to address identified needs;
Creating an identity of the Collaborative throughout the community.

The collaborative meets monthly and has four working committees to support its role:

- A steering committee, which serves as the leadership of the collaborative;
- A data committee, which is responsible for obtaining data and best-practice information and for compiling a comprehensive community-wide resource directory of all area reading programs in order to identify gaps and opportunities for further collaboration, so programs can be better coordinated and supported through more volunteers and finances;
- A resource committee, which is responsible for researching and obtaining resources to support the work of the collaborative, such as completing a $3.5 million Early Reading First federal grant application; and
- A marketing committee.

Improving the reading skills of our youth is a community challenge—everyone can play a role, and everyone has a stake. This is a business issue, not just a social issue. It affects the economy of the community. The next section looks at some direct results, after only a year's time, of this collaboration of various education and business entities.

EARLY READING FIRST (ERF) GRANT INITIATIVE

As a result of dividing into the various subcommittees, the need for funding came to the forefront. The Bakersfield City schools had just recently sought grant monies from the new federal program, Reading First. The Reading First grant initiative inspired members of the group to look into other sources of funding, and the Early Reading First federal grant initiative was discovered.

The grant-writing process required many meetings of representatives from various agencies brainstorming ideas as to how a project could be conceived under the Early Reading First guidelines. After several initial meetings, a team of three completed the grant proposal: a Bakersfield City

School district grant writer; the School Readiness program director from the Kern County Superintendent of Schools office; and a California State University, Bakersfield, literacy professor. This combination of city, county, and state educational institutions offered a blend of knowledge and skills required by this very explicit and technical grant-writing process. The initial proposal was submitted by March 2003. Over six hundred proposals were submitted throughout the country. Kern County's grant was one of 125 to be invited to submit a full proposal, and although we did not receive funding, the application process put in place an excellent team that will submit other proposals in the future.

PILOT PROJECT—THE BAKERSFIELD EARLY LITERACY LEARNING ADVANTAGE (BELLA)

Knowing the ERF grant might not be funded, but excited about beginning a preschool project, plans were made by the grant-writing team to do a pilot project—just in case. Attempts were under way before the grant announcements were made to implement Plan B. In Plan B, outside funding would be garnered to provide a modified version of the grant application model. In this model, professional development would be provided directly to the state preschool teachers by area literacy experts in Bakersfield City and surrounding area schools. Rather than housing literacy experts in each of five sites, current preschool teachers, whose qualifications may only require twenty-four course units, will be trained in early reading acquisition skills and assessments. An early literacy course offering to be included in the coursework for preschool teachers at the local community college is being developed. Bakersfield City School District preschool program specialists were brought into the beginning of the process of implementing Plan B. Members of the Target Reading First collaborative will be called upon for financial and volunteer assistance.

READING PROGRAM DATA COLLECTION

Another aspect of the work of the Target Reading First Reading Collaborative is the compilation of a comprehensive community-wide resource directory of all area reading programs to identify gaps and opportunities for further collaboration and to be better coordinated and supported through more volunteers and finances. After-school programs, book give-aways, community volunteer reading in the schools, and new books for new parents are just a few of the many projects being carried out by area agencies, organizations, and businesses. The directory will be a way to tie together those who need the services and those who would like to participate in providing them. California State University, Bakersfield, is providing an internship for a student to collect this data, begin the evaluation of the programs, and prepare the information for a website sponsored by the Reading Collaborative. The internship could lead to a research document that would become a master's in literacy student thesis.

PUBLIC SCHOOL/UNIVERSITY TEACHER EDUCATION

Another outgrowth of the business/education/community partnership that the Target Reading First Collaborative can be credited for is linking up university reading credential professors at California State University, Bakersfield, with Reading First grant schools. The director of the Reading First initiative in the Bakersfield City schools presented information to a Reading Collaborative meeting on the initial work being done in the fifteen school sites that qualified to receive Reading First assistance. Similar to the Early Reading First proposal, these fifteen schools each had a qualified reading specialist assigned to it to model strategies, work with classroom teachers, complete assessments, and make recommendations based on those assessments. The difficult task that the Reading First Director is trying to implement is to find ways to help teachers group flexibly for reading and spelling instruction. This particular classroom management method is being taught in local university reading methods classes. The Reading First director and a university literacy professor, a member of the collaborative, have teamed up to promote this method of teaching so that preservice teachers can not only learn about flexible grouping but also see it in action. Thus, a ready-made source of pretrained teachers is able to enter the Reading First schools armed with the knowledge and the experience required.

EDUCATION/BUSINESS PARTNERSHIP
FOR A PRESCHOOL PILOT PROGRAM

The following article from the *Bakersfield Californian* details another project that has also come directly from Reading Collaborative connections:

Program Seeks to Prepare Children
by Tim Bragg, Californian *staff writer*

A wake-up call is not what many parents of kindergartners expect when they go for the first "Back to School Night" meeting. But that's often what they get, said former kindergarten teacher Margie Berumen, now a vice principal at Planz Elementary School.

"They would say, 'all we did was play with blocks and eat graham crackers and milk when I was in kindergarten,'" Berumen said. "Now, students in kindergarten are learning things like how to form simple words. Things have changed."

With state standards increasing the academic content of kindergarten courses, educators say children need to be better prepared.

That's why a group of Kern County educators and business people have formed a committee to develop a pre-kindergarten education program, one that can be used as a model by other schools in Kern County.

"The expectations for kindergartners are what we had been expecting of first-graders a few years ago," said Wendy Wayne, division administrator for child development and family services at the Kern County Superintendent of Schools office and a member of the project's steering committee.

The committee's work is still in the preliminary stages: Decisions on the program's curriculum, format and funding have yet to be made. A final version of the program is several years away, at least.

But a pilot program, involving a partnership between the Kern County Superintendent of Schools and Greenfield and Rosedale union school districts, ran a test run over the summer.

The Greenfield Union School District tested the basic concept for some incoming kindergartners at two elementary schools this summer.

The results of the test run are still being analyzed, said Greenfield Union Superintendent Gary Rice, another member of the steering committee.

But he said anecdotal evidence from kindergarten teachers suggests the classes made the incoming pupils who participated better prepared for kindergarten.

"If children are not academically prepared for kindergarten, there is a domino effect that occurs," Rice said. "If they are behind on certain basic skills, then they have a hard time learning more advanced skills in the upper grades.

"By the time they are in the seventh or eighth grade, they've failed so many times they have a bad attitude about learning," he said. "That affects their performance in high school."

Wayne said the idea for the kindergarten preparation programs started on two fronts.

Some officials from the superintendent of schools office held focus groups with kindergarten teachers to see what skills incoming pupils should possess.

Also around that time, part of the Vision 20/20 group, a gathering of community members who brainstormed ideas to improve Bakersfield, began to think about ways to improve the academic skills of high school graduates to achieve a better trained work force for the future.

Employers sometimes find their job candidates lack some basic skills needed for employment.

"We want our work force to have strong reading and writing skills, and math skills that include an awareness of algebra," said Susan Hersberger, public affairs director for Aera Energy LLC, who also works on the steering committee.

Eventually, a committee to develop the prekindergarten program was formed with the superintendent's office, and representatives from the two school districts, the Kern County Network for Children, Bakersfield College, Cal State Bakersfield, Aera Energy LLC, Jim Burke Ford, Kern Schools Federal Credit Union and The Californian.

Wayne said the planning group hopes to continue with another test run in the summer of 2004.

Although some private and government-sponsored preschools offer childhood development and prekindergarten programs, there are enough children who fall through the cracks for the county's effort to be worthwhile, said Alice Johnson, assistant superintendent for curriculum at the Rosedale Union School District.

"As always, you get children coming into kindergarten with a variety of backgrounds. Some have had preschool classes and some haven't," Johnson said. "This will help the kids who are behind the others."

The Target Reading First Collaborative has been in full operation for more than a year. Monthly meetings provide a forum for sharing community- and school-based literacy projects and ongoing educational presentations about literacy acquisition. In addition, the connections that have been made among the members and other concerned residents have been invaluable. Over time, the Target Reading First Collaborative will make a significant difference in this community, and it expects to show significant long-term results to both the education and business communities. Fortunately, there is no lack of interest or energy to accomplish these goals.

NOTE

1. Kern County Department of Social Services, *Report Card 2003: Examining Issues Affecting Kern County's Children*.

19

How Parents Can Help Develop Safe Schools

Today's schools are serving children from dysfunctional homes, children living in poverty, children of teenage parents, and special education students. Unfortunately, resources to adequately serve the total range of needs presented by these students are becoming increasingly limited. Adequate parental supervision and control of these students has weakened, and many students have diminished respect for all forms of authority, including the authority of school personnel. There is an imperative need for schools to identify tools, strategies, and model programs that enhance the safety and success of all children and the professionals who serve them.

Because young people are legally required to attend school, school personnel have a corresponding duty to provide children with a safe, secure, and peaceful environment in which learning can occur. Achieving this end requires that every school district and each individual school develop a school safety plan. Development of such plans is not limited to the school alone but must necessarily involve the entire community. The "Safe Schools" materials presented at the start of this chapter as an example of such a plan are taken from the North Central Regional Educational Laboratory (www.ncrel.org).

A SAFE-SCHOOL PLAN

A safe-school plan is an all-encompassing program that provides for the safety and security of students and educators. It is an ongoing, systematic, and comprehensive process that addresses both short-term and long-term safety measures to eliminate violent attitudes and behaviors in the school. Its basic goal is to create and maintain a positive and welcoming school climate in which all members take pride. This climate is free of drugs, gangs, violence, intimidation, fear, and shaming. A healthy, positive school climate promotes the emotional well-being and growth of every student, while providing a safe, secure environment that does not condone violence in any form. At the same time, however, the school provides firm and consistent rules and guidelines for appropriate student behavior.

Each of the stakeholders involved in the school should recognize his or her responsibility to work for and achieve the following goals.

School Administrator Goals

- Administrators provide leadership in assessing, developing, and monitoring the safe-school plan.
- Administrators establish a continuous system of school crime tracking, reporting, and feedback, and provide this information to concerned parties.
- Administrators design a school environment that ensures safe traffic patterns within and to and from school.
- Administrators adopt procedures for emergency evacuation and crisis management.
- Administrators establish a school safety council or school planning team with representatives from school staff, students, parents, and community representatives. This council is responsible for providing advice and making decisions about critically important cases of violence and crime, evaluating the state of school safety, and proposing revisions to the school discipline code and school safety plan as deemed necessary.
- Administrators ensure that all people involved with the school are working in support of safe schools. This goal involves parental involvement, careful screening and selection of all staff members, inservice training on school crime for all staff, comprehensive violence-prevention approaches, intervention in bullying behavior as well as racial and sexual harassment, addressing of student discipline issues in a non-shaming but firm manner that does not incite violent behavior,

and development of interagency partnerships directed at creating a safe school within a safe community.

- Administrators provide leadership in developing extracurricular activities and recreation programs that provide positive alternatives to juvenile crime and violence, along with specific programs directed at eliminating gang influence in schools and preventing school drug trafficking.
- Administrators provide leadership in developing a school discipline code of student behavior and conduct. Such a code requires the input of parents, students, teachers, youth-serving professionals, and community leaders.

Teacher Goals

- Teachers respond to students in a caring and non-shaming manner. They also provide consistent and firm guidelines and rules regarding student behavior.
- Teachers consider the teaching and modeling of pro-social behavior to be as important as the teaching of academic subjects.
- Teachers display diligent and impartial behavior when supervising students. They use a consistent and prompt manner to grant rewards for good behavior and sanctions for unacceptable behavior. Teachers participate in the development of a school safety plan, discipline code, and racial and sexual harassment policy. They also play a responsible part in the implementation of such policies by promptly and consistently reporting incidents of misbehavior, crime, violence, and harassment.

Parent Goals

- Parents are equal partners with administrators and teachers in the development of the school safety plan and discipline code. Their recommendations on policy and implementation are carefully considered.
- Parents are familiar with the school safety plan and the school discipline code.
- Parents are responsible for monitoring the behavior of their sons and daughters.

Student Goals

- Students want—and are entitled to—a safe, orderly school environment in which to learn.
- Students develop a sense of responsibility for contributing to the improvement of school order and safety. Members of all peer groups participate actively in the planning, implementation, and enforcement of discipline policy and programs.

HOW PARENTS CAN IMPROVE THEIR CHILD'S PERFORMANCE BY REDUCING ALCOHOL AND OTHER DRUG USE

The rest of the chapter, written by the author, argues that to reduce substance abuse, parents should work with school districts to develop policy statements that focus on school-based prevention and refer treatment to other agencies in the community. The chapter includes background about the field, information about how to use the Students-at-Risk software and materials with your child to prevent dropout and substance abuse, curricular programs to reduce abuse within schools, a community involvement program, a law enforcement program, information on how to assess the extent of adolescent substance abuse, and strategies for parents to use at home.

Background

Most states have developed guidelines to assist school districts in formulating substance abuse policies. Typical guidelines include a philosophy of school-based prevention, a focus on dissemination of effective program descriptions, emphasis on affective as well as cognitive measures for prevention, stress on the importance of peer and family relationships, and strategies utilizing career and life planning. Suggestions for implementing a comprehensive school-based prevention program focus on curriculum design, in-service training, staffing, counseling, and parent and community involvement.

In the area of alcohol and other drug prevention, school policy and procedure is developed from state and federal guidelines, reaction of substance use incidents in the school, and recommendations of community and administrative planning committees. However the policies evolve, it is important to review them periodically at a school and district level. For example, some school policies developed in the 1960s did not specify a clear "no use" message of alcohol and other drugs. This is important, as history has taught us that we often get what we expect to get. Also, policies can best serve the students and the school system by clearly reflecting the goals and philosophy and by setting norms and standards for all staff and students to that end. With this framework, the policy should be proactive and specific within the limits of legal parameters.

Developing a Clear Prevention Policy

A prevention policy that applies to students and staff sets the tone for a district to address alcohol and other drug (AOD) issues directly and humanely. A clear policy helps all understand the district's expectations and accept the position that the consequences are equitable. A clear policy can also provide motivation for staff and students to seek assistance for AOD problems.

A prevention policy is proactive when it

enhances and supports student development;

encourages schools to link with community agencies for needed services not provided;

coordinates messages with other district policy and procedure for at-risk students;

assists self-referring students without punishment;

provides resource information to encourage school staff to seek treatment and requires AOD problem staff to participate in treatment; and

addresses prevention policy needs in the areas of staff development, curriculum, student support services, parent education and involvement, community involvement, and evaluation.

A prevention policy must clearly address several issues with standards and procedure. For example, guidelines should specify how the policy and intervention program are to be implemented, and procedures need to be developed that help the program function smoothly and provide reinforcement to participating students.

The policy needs a strong legal foundation to ensure that participating staff will be supported in their prevention efforts when they work within these legal parameters. The legal parameters include abiding by state and federal laws related to drug and alcohol use and should be reviewed by legal counsel.

Developing a school district prevention policy includes the following steps:

1. Educate and create awareness.
2. Establish a district philosophy.
3. Form a working group.
4. Develop common language and common goals.
5. Create a philosophy statement.
6. Draft the policy.
7. Submit for board approval.
8. Disseminate the policy.
9. Review, update, and redisseminate the policy annually.

The policy regulations and procedures are developed either with the policy or shortly after so that the roles and responsibilities of school personnel implementing the prevention policy are clear. Disciplinary regulations and procedures that traditionally emphasize punishment, usually suspension, may be revised to include constructive alternatives, such as mandatory participation in workshops, support groups, assessment, or counseling.

The student support system developed is dependent on the resources and administrative style of the school district. The roles and responsibilities of identification, preassessment, and referral of students may be shared between school staff, consultants, and community resources. Most programs have the following components:

• Initial intervention strategies for classroom teachers who become concerned about a student
• A system of collecting information from several sources on students regarding AOD risk factors
• A system of reviewing and evaluating the referral information and determining the action needed

- Strategies for involving and motivating parents, students, and school staff to support the intervention plan
- A system for monitoring the progress of students referred for intervention

Parent Counseling Software

This counseling and discussion tool is designed to heighten students' awareness of a possible likelihood for dropout or substance dependency. The program is produced by Students-at-Risk (SAR) to predict dropout and substance abuse (see appendix B). This program establishes a reference point at which parents or school staff may open discussions with students who may be at risk. The intent of this program is not to predict dependency or label individuals. Properly used, it will assist parents or school counselors with the task of helping the students recognize their individual potential for dependency or dropout. This program is intended for use by parents or school staff who have talked with the school staff member who is most knowledgeable about dropout and substance abuse prevention. The program runs on PC hardware using the Windows operating system.

The following questions are used in the software designed for secondary students:

1. How often is the student angry?
2. How many of the student's friends use alcohol or drugs?
3. How many close adults (relatives or friends) use alcohol or drugs frequently?
4. How many times has the student been high or drunk?
5. Is the student's family against drugs?
6. How often do the student's parents know where he or she is?
7. Would the student use drugs or alcohol if a friend dared him or her?
8. How many times has the student been arrested?
9. Has the student ever been suspended or expelled?
10. How many D's or F's did the student get on the last report card?
11. Does the student have a juvenile delinquency record?
12. Does the student have a certified disability?
13. How many times was the student absent last semester?
14. Did the student move or change schools last year?

CURRENT INTERVENTION STRATEGIES IN SUBURBAN UNIFIED

A school district that has successfully incorporated a prevention policy into its programs is Suburban Unified.

Elementary Programs:

1. DARE (Drug Abuse Resistance Education)
2. Babes, Babes' Kids
3. Project Self-Esteem
4. Developmental Kindergarten
5. Saturday School

K–12 Programs:

6. CASA—Very active drug and alcohol effort by parents, students, and staff.
7. PRIDE—Parent to Parent Networking
8. Red Ribbon Week, Awareness Weeks
9. Categorical Programs (Chapter I, GATE, ESL, etc.)
10. Summer School Program
11. "Successful Parents for Successful Kids" Conference
12. Migrant Education Program
13. School Study Teams
14. Special Education Programs, I.E.P. Teams
15. Gang Information Workshops
16. Good Working Relationship with the Orange Police Dept.
17. SARB (School Attendance Review Board)
18. Quest International (Skills Programs)
19. Home and Hospital
20. Independent Study Program
21. Co-curricular Programs (Clubs, Student Government, etc.)

Secondary Programs:

22. PAL (Peer Assistance Leadership)
23. Athletic Programs
24. Choices Program
25. Pregnant Minor Program

26. Child Development Program
27. Continuation High School Program
28. Middle School Philosophy (Homeroom, Interdisciplinary Teams, Child Centered, etc.)
29. Regional Occupation Program (ROP)
30. Opportunity Class (Grades 7–9)
31. Work Experience Programs
32. Decision Making Skills Class
33. Summer Recreation Program
34. Rancho Santiago Evening Programs
35. Hispanic Youth, Leadership Conference
36. Career Day, College and University Nights
37. Academy Program (High School)

LAW ENFORCEMENT COLLABORATION

Substance abuse has reached epidemic proportions in many communities, and administrators will find police and other law enforcement agencies ready to collaborate in many ways to reduce abuse. One nationally known effort is Project DARE (Drug Abuse Resistance Education). This program was developed by the Los Angeles Police Department in collaboration with the Los Angeles Unified School District. It covers grades 5 through 12 and consists of seventeen lessons taught by district-trained police officers on full-time duty with the project.

The lessons include the following topics: Practices for Personal Safety; Drug Use and Misuse; Consequences of Using or Choosing Not to Use Drugs; Resisting Pressure to Use Drugs; Resistance Techniques: Ways to Say No; Building Self-Esteem; Assertiveness: How to Exercise Your Rights without Interfering with Others' Rights; Managing Stress without Taking Drugs; Media Influences on Drug Use; Decision Making and Risk Taking; Alternatives to Drug Abuse; Alternative Activities; An Officer-Planned Lesson for a Particular Class; Role Modeling: A Visit by a High School Student Who Is a Positive Role Model; Summarizing and Assessing Learning; Composing Essays or Writing Letters on How to Respond to Pressure to Use Drugs; and Schoolwide Assembly to Award DARE Students Their Certificates of Achievement.

ASSESSING ADOLESCENT SUBSTANCE USE

In the field of substance abuse surveys here are some tips in carrying out surveys to find out if your situation is improving:

1. Identify who will use your survey information and the minimum information they need.
2. Secret-response items should be considered in a brief survey.
3. Keep the survey as simple as possible.
4. Report percentages, not complex statistics.
5. Identify the proportion of at-risk respondents.
6. Stay with your first instrument for year-after-year consistency.
7. Compare your results with state and national figures.
8. Never report results so comparisons between schools or districts can be made.
9. Provide confidential reports to principals and teachers.

We turn now to strategies for use by parents, who are so often the key to reducing abuse for young people.

PARENT STRATEGIES

Parents should take responsibility to identify agencies in the community that can help them if they suspect a child is a potential abuser. In addition, they can become involved in the following ways:

- Discuss issues with children early.
- Discuss issues with other parents.
- Know where children are when they are out of the home.
- Support children in developing friendships with other responsible adults.
- Practice social skills, such as those involved in clarifying communication, in the home.
- Take classes and be active in local substance abuse prevention groups.

- Know the early warning signs of substance.
- Confront children in a caring and concerned fashion, as needed.

SCHOOL STRATEGIES

Ocean View School District in Huntington Beach, California, has a model for developing a district or school drug prevention program that has been recognized at the national level for its fine approach. A successful program like Ocean View's

- Is age-appropriate
- Reaches across the K–12 curriculum
- Focuses on self-esteem enhancement
- Teaches decision-making skills
- Provides opportunities for parent and youth involvement—put them to work
- Has serious evaluation, both process and product
- Includes school, religious, community, business, media, public and private agency, and police involvement

In summary, the role of the school is central in the battle to reduce substance abuse. It includes focus on curriculum design, in-service training, staffing, counseling, and parent and community involvement.

20

Helping People Change

This chapter presents a model for helping parents, teachers, and administrators accomplish the tasks that need attention. People tend to change for one of three reasons: First, they are dissatisfied with their level of success in some area; they want to improve. Second, they think others disapprove of their present behavior. Finally, they see a way to behave and work that is easier and more effective than what they have been doing. Usually they come to the decision to change when they see someone behave or work in a way that they think can work for them.

This change implementation model is based on the assumption that an individual can change her or his behavior in a systematic fashion if there is strong motivation and support from that person's significant other—which might be a spouse or another parent.

There are identifiable mechanisms for making change using three categories:

- *Unfreezing*, or creating motivation for change
- *Changing*, or developing new responses based upon new information
- *Refreezing*, or stabilizing and integrating change

Each stage results from the person' response to certain activities that can produce change. In unfreezing, the person may move to readiness for change through a lack of confirmation of his or her previously operating self-image. A teacher might, for instance, want to be the "best math teacher in the school." She might become ready for change through beginning to feel inadequacy or failure in herself. Unfreezing may also occur through the removal of self-imposed barriers that have prevented change.

Unfreezing involves an emotional or attitudinal shift that we might call "readiness to change." Attitudes can be cognitive or emotional at their source. *Cognitive* attitudes are not deeply ingrained and can be altered by new information. *Emotional* attitudes connect to our values and are not so easily changed. If you had an anti-education value, you probably would not have read this book. On the other hand, you as a parent may not be willing to spend much time at your child's school, but you might be willing to read the arguments for doing more. If this is true, new information might allow you to change your behavior. Change occurs when we locate information from some credible source, redefine the situation in terms we find sensible, and make the decision to alter our behavior.

Refreezing occurs when we integrate new responses into our personality and into significant personal relationships. You might become ready for change through beginning to feel you can gain new respect from your friends. Refreezing occurs when we integrate new responses into our personality and into significant personal relationships.

Here is the model for change:

Mark your choices in rank based on what you feel you would do to change your behavior.

Unfreeezing
To create a readiness to change, I will:

1. Try to analyze my behavior and see if I find some insight in the area of concern.
2. Do my best to remove a barrier that is preventing change.
3. Examine what other parents (teachers/administrators) I respect are doing in order to see possibilities.

Changing
To assist in the change process, I have:

1. Worked to identify questionable assumptions and beliefs.
2. Developed new definitions or broadened my frame of reference.

3. Changed my criteria for making a judgment.
4. Talked to my significant other about the need to change.
5. Developed alternatives that make sense for me.
6. Selected an alternative and made my decision to change.

Refreezing

The process of refreezing after change is essentially one of becoming comfortable with one's new approach to the situation. To accomplish this, we need to integrate our changed behavior into our lives as new responses within our personality, as well as making them part of our important personal relationships. To assist in integrating these new behaviors I have:

1. Worked to see that the new behavior and attitudes are integrated in a thoughtful way with my general behavior and attitudes.
2. Asked my friends to help me see if my new behavior and attitudes are on target and are taking me where I want to go.
3. Considered unfreezing the new behaviors and attitudes so I can start over and do a better job at integrating the new and old behaviors and attitudes.

This model, in its present form or adapted to fit your situation, will be of valuable assistance as you go through the change process.

21

The Skagit County Best PLACE Collaboration

Margaret Thompson

The Best PLACE (People and Literacy Achieving Community Enrichment) Program has, in its third year, successfully established and administered a wide variety of highly needed literacy projects within the Skagit County, Washington, area, utilizing a $19 million 21st Century grant from the U.S. Department of Education. The program continues to stand as an example of how key organizations within a community can work together to make a difference for children and their families. Several factors can be used to demonstrate our effectiveness. Among others, we have met or exceeded our goals in all areas for the first three years as outlined in our original proposal. We are progressing toward the development of a long-range sustainability plan that will keep our program operating for many years to come.

Best PLACE targets infants to adults with literacy-based programs that serve the entire family in a variety of ways. Our early learning program, with fourteen centers in full operation, has served close to 1,200 children in the past three years. This comprehensive program has built-in elements that connect families and prepare children for school success while providing a safe and nurturing environment. No similar programs were available on school district properties prior to the 21st Century grant award.

A summer program that serves close to 1,800 elementary-aged children has been expanded through grant support. Furthermore, a strong literacy focus has become a central curricular goal for the summer activities. As a result, we have been able to measure substantial academic gains for children who participated in the eight-week summer program for the past three years.

Best PLACE has teamed up with several existing community organizations and school districts in setting up and expanding after-school programs. Currently, over five hundred students in twenty-three classrooms
across the county have access to this type of assistance. These programs
serve students in academic areas as well as recreation, arts, enrichment,
and homework support. We are already close to achieving our three-year
goal for the after-school program.

The establishment of our teen programs can stand as an example of the
collaborative relationships that we have created with a variety of organizations such as the YMCA, Boys and Girls Clubs, Salvation Army, Parks
and Recreation, Youth and Family Services, and others. We have worked
with these organizations on evaluating needs and spearheading much-
needed new services for youth at risk of school failure. These programs
are now serving over three thousand teens in Skagit Valley, far exceeding
our goal for direct services to this segment of the population for the first
three years of our program.

Prior to the Best PLACE Program, there was virtually no adult literacy
program in Skagit County. During the past three years, we have served close
to four hundred adults a year and established eleven sites where we are operating adult learning centers throughout the county. These centers, staffed
primarily by volunteer tutors and AmeriCorps participants, are located in
schools and community buildings. We believe that the number of people
seeking adult literacy will continue to grow. We have recently established
multiaged centers where all members of the family can receive services at
one location and also receive free child care, greatly enhancing our program. This focus on family literacy has added depth to our program and
helps us reach our goal of supporting and serving families in our county.

While we continue to be proud of our accomplishments when it comes
to establishing new programs and services, we are cognizant of the need
to set the highest quality and accountability standards for our community
involvement. All of our programs are based on widely accepted research
and best practices in the various component areas. In addition, we have
built-in assessment procedures aimed at providing feedback with regard
to the effectiveness of our program and the organization of our project.

Best PLACE will, in the coming year, increasingly focus its efforts on providing opportunities for literacy development for the entire family. We are administering programs that will allow access to service independent of potential barriers such as language, income level, and transportation. Ultimately,

we want to increase literacy activities in the homes and provide a support structure that can be accessed in the neighborhoods where people live.

The Best PLACE Project has positively impacted the lives of hundreds of families within Skagit County in the past three years. As we continue to look for ways to sustain our project after the grant term, we will be relying on our partners to be the "key champions" for our sustainability efforts. As we work together to build our long-range plan, we will consider the unique contributions of our partners and continue to identify strategies to garner needed resources.

As our original grant proposal stated, ultimately we hope to create a multifaceted community support system that will help sustain family literacy and provide a large-scale replicable model for improving the future of children and families, thereby strengthening our communities. In our third year of grant activity, we are well on our way to achieving this lofty goal.

Burnett describes four levels of collaboration that are essential in ensuring successful school-linked services:[1]

Collaboration between administrators provides the support and impetus for a successful program.

Collaboration between social service providers and school personnel ensures that the program is adequately planned and designed and that it runs smoothly on a day-to-day basis.

Collaboration among members of a participating agency ensures responsibility, trust, direction, and an atmosphere of collegiality.

Collaboration among teachers, social service providers, and families is essential because services are actually delivered at this level. In most cases, teachers already have a relationship with the parents and are able to act as intermediaries in getting services to the families.

In addition to the fine effort in Skagit County, Washington, one of the best examples of serious collaboration we have found is in Illinois between the Teachers Academy and several school districts. Their report summarizes their success story.

The Teachers Academy for Mathematics and Science[2]

Overview

The Teachers Academy for Mathematics and Science has raised students' math and science scores among six of the lowest achieving school districts in Illinois. Statewide, TAMS has served 128 schools and 3,600 teachers in its intensive program. Thousands of additional teachers have participated in technology and science education activities. TAMS has brought $73.6 million in additional funding to schools in Illinois.

Rigorous ongoing research allows us to document the Academy's effect on student achievement.

MS Experience

The Teachers Academy for Mathematics and Science includes:

Chicago Public Schools
Elgin Public Schools
Aurora Public Schools
Joliet Public Schools
East St. Louis Public Schools
Cahokia Public Schools

How do we know the Academy is effective?

By comparing Academy schools to non-Academy schools inthe six districts.

The percentage of students meeting or exceeding state standards at Academy schools rose 17.4 percent from 1999 to 2001; at non-Academy schools it rose 13.3 percent.

What we've learned about professional development

Many teachers do not have the minimum competencies they need to enable their students to meet state and national standards. Raising student achievement requires improving teachers' knowledge and classroom practices. A critical mass of teachers (at least 80 percent) must attend an intensive, long-term standards-based program to realize and sustain improvement in test scores.

For the program to be most effective, district superintendents, principals and teachers must understand the goals and work to implement changes. Teaching materials must be made available for use in the classroom.

NOTES

1. See William Callison, www.ncrel.org/sdrs/areas/issues/envrnmnt/css/cs11k15.htm; accessed September 25, 2003.

2. See www.tams.org/resource_assests/410/statewide%presentation.pdf; accessed October 29, 2003.

Appendix A

One Hundred Ways to Be Involved in Your Child's Education

The following list of suggestions is based on the National Standards for Parent/Family Involvement Program's *100 Ways for Parents to Be Involved in Their Child's Education* from the National Parent Teachers Organization. You may contact them by phone at (800) 307-4PTA, by e-mail at info@pta.org, and on their website, www.pta.org.

1. Give positive feedback and show appreciation for teachers and the principal.
2. Approach interactions with a positive attitude and an open mind.
3. Listen to others' viewpoints.
4. Share your child's strengths, talents, and interests with your child's teachers.
5. Share expectations and set goals together for your child.
6. Make appointments as needed to discuss your child's progress or concerns.
7. Attend parent–teacher conferences with specific questions you want to ask.
8. Indicate the best way for the school to give you information (phone, e-mail, notes, etc.).
9. Understand and reinforce school rules and expectations at home.
10. Participate in informal opportunities to talk with and get to know school staff and educators.

11. Address concerns or questions honestly, openly, and early on.
12. Attend PTA or parent meetings regularly.
13. Read classroom and/or school newsletters.
14. Visit your school's web page.
15. Know school staff's extensions and office hours.
16. Read and know your school's handbook.
17. Request that information be available in all relevant languages.
18. Share your family's culture, values, and parenting practices with your child's school.
19. Share your perceptions with educators and school staff of how parents are treated.
20. Work with school staff and educators to revise and improve perceptions and school climate.
21. Meet your child's friends and get to know their parents.
22. Contact your school for information on family programs and resources.
23. Help establish a parent center at school and use its resources.
24. Help create a toy/book lending library and visit it regularly.
25. Assist in developing parent support programs/groups and attend them.
26. Attend workshops or seminars on various parenting topics.
27. Participate in parenting classes on child development, expectations, discipline, and so on.
28. Attend parent fairs and other events especially for parents and families.
29. Start a parent book club to discuss current publications.
30. Help create and/or contribute to a school newsletter on parenting.
31. Assist in creating and/or offer your services to before- and after-school programs.
32. Build a child file with medical records, pictures, fingerprints, and other items.
33. Make donations and/or offer to work at clothing drives or swaps, food co-ops, and the like.
34. Ask teachers or counselors about how to talk with your children about tough topics.
35. Discuss your child's school day and homework daily.

36. Learn your child's strengths and weaknesses in different areas of school.
37. Provide a quiet, well-lighted place with basic school supplies for studying/homework.
38. Help your children break down projects into smaller, more manageable steps.
39. Develop a consistent daily routine and time for studying and homework.
40. Provide encouragement and approval for effort and schoolwork.
41. Share your interests, hobbies, and talents with your children.
42. Provide children with books, magazines, and so forth, and develop a nighttime reading routine.
43. View selected TV programs together and then review and discuss them.
44. Make family trips to the library, zoo, museum, or park a fun learning experience.
45. Talk with your child's teacher on creating home learning games and activities.
46. Complete interactive homework assignments with your child.
47. Attend meetings on learning expectations, assessment, and grading procedures.
48. Help set goals and develop a personalized education plan for your child.
49. Participate in activities that help you understand school technology.
50. Help plan and attend family nights on improving study habits, doing homework, and other parent–child activities.
51. Help develop, visit, or offer services to your school's study/tutor center.
52. Participate in fairs and fests for math, science, history, and so forth.
53. Respond to school surveys on your interests, talents, and skills.
54. Let school staff know your availability to volunteer (days, times, and how often).
55. Supervise and coordinate evening and weekend volunteer activities at school.
56. Assist your child's teacher in the classroom or on field trips when you are able.

57. Work with school staff and teachers to develop volunteer activities you can do from home.
58. Assist school staff and educators in creating a warm and welcoming atmosphere for parents.
59. Help provide child care and/or transportation for volunteering parents.
60. Help develop creative ways to use volunteers at school.
61. Actively help school staff recruit parents and community members as volunteers.
62. Attend training and orientation on how to be an effective volunteer.
63. Learn and uphold school discipline, confidentiality, and other policies as a volunteer.
64. Plan a regular time each week to talk with school staff and educators with whom you are working.
65. Help develop volunteer job descriptions and evaluations.
66. Participate in organizing and planning ways to recognize and appreciate volunteers.
67. Respond to school surveys/questionnaires on how effective volunteer programs are.
68. Help develop and distribute a volunteer directory to parents, school staff, and teachers.
69. Provide volunteer consulting services to school staff or educators in your areas of expertise.
70. Learn of school and district policies and practices that affect children.
71. Voice your support or concerns on any issue that will affect your family.
72. Be involved in decisions on student placement and course and textbook selections.
73. Participate in meetings to determine special educational needs and services.
74. Attend workshops on problem solving, conflict resolution, public speaking, and so forth.
75. Serve on school advisory councils or committees on curriculum, discipline, and so forth.
76. Serve on a site-based school management team with teachers and the principal.

77. Encourage and support older children in serving in student leadership positions.
78. Help your school create a student's rights and responsibilities guide for families.
79. Attend PTA, school board, and/or town meetings and speak to issues of concern.
80. Learn representatives' backgrounds and participate in school board elections.
81. Work with teachers and school administrators to develop a parent involvement policy.
82. Write, call, or travel to state capitals to support or oppose proposed legislation.
83. Participate in petition drives or letter-writing campaigns to Congress on legislation.
84. Give testimony at public hearings in support of or opposition to education legislation.
85. Vote in local, state, and federal elections for public officials who support education.
86. Help your school develop a directory of social and community services.
87. Find out information on community resources and organizations and use them.
88. Help develop and/or distribute a community newsletter to local agencies and businesses.
89. Help coordinate and participate in an event to raise money for a local charity.
90. Talk with employers about holding parent meetings or parenting workshops on-site.
91. Advocate for flexible work schedules and leave time to attend school functions.
92. Encourage employers and local businesses to make donations and support school programs.
93. Help organize and/or participate in community health fairs.
94. Help recruit community members (seniors, business people) to volunteer at school.
95. Become active in community groups such as YMCA and Boy and Girl Scouts.

96. Serve on local community advisory councils and committees.
97. Work with local authorities and public officials to sponsor community events.
98. Help organize and/or participate in a community "clean-up" or "beautification" project.
99. Encourage and help facilitate your child's participation in community service.
100. Be a role model: be active in community service yourself or together with your child.

Appendix B

Secondary Risk Assessment

$\mathbf{P}$lease select the questions you wish to use and make a list of them for students and/or parents to use as a questionnaire.

1. The interventions suggested are in order of intensity, low requiring the least intensive intervention, and high the most intensive.
2. You as the teacher can often provide most low responses as a part of your usual and expected interactions with students and parents. Medium responses can often be planned and carried out by two teachers working together. High interventions can be discussed with your principal for suggestions of who might help.
3. In every instance that the response to the risk assessment questionnaire has triggered a suggested intervention (one of the three listed areas of concern), it is strongly recommended that you make at least a low response, which typically means a one-to-one interview with the student.
4. Low interventions will suggest an individual meeting or interview with the student to gather more information. Suggestions for discussion will be offered later in this manual. The low interview will help ascertain whether medium or high interventions might also be beneficial.
5. Medium interventions may suggest ongoing support to monitor the student's situation. Typically you should discuss a medium intervention with another teacher who can help you develop a plan to help the student.

6. Your principal may suggest that when you have a student with high need for interventions you may ask a resource person for some help.

7. It is important for educators to use their knowledge and experience in interpreting the student responses during a one-on-one interview.

For example, question 1 asks, "How often is the student angry?" The responses include "never," "sometimes," "frequently," and "very frequently." What one student considers frequently may seem to peers and teachers to be very frequently or, on the other hand, to be only sometimes. It all depends on the student's frame of reference. In deciding what level of intervention is necessary, it is helpful to look at what you know of— and can learn about—the student.

THE QUESTIONNAIRE AND SUGGESTED INTERVENTIONS

Question 1

How often is the student angry?

Low

Interview the student for reasons, to select the appropriate intervention(s).

First, establish a caring and helpful environment/relationship with the student so that the student will trust you to give you information.

You may share some information about yourself, that you care about students, that you experienced some challenging times growing up— whatever may be appropriate.

Suggestions for discussion topics include these: Tell me about your day. Is there a particular time of the day you notice anger? Is there a particular situation/person (teacher, peer, parent, important relationship, etc.) that triggers anger for you? Have you gone through any family or relationship changes in the last few years?

This initial interview may show you what additional interventions, if any, are needed. For example, if a student's anger is a result of inadequate social skills, identifying and teaching particular skills may be helpful. If the anger is due to a family crisis, other responses will be more appropriate (see examples later).

Medium

If indicated by information gathered in the interview, work with another teacher to provide ongoing support and monitoring of the student's situation. This might involve helping with schoolwork or other problems, sending a birthday card and other little notes, and doing occasional activities together.

Medium interventions may also include informal discussion and brainstorming of alternative behaviors and teaching of social skills or self-esteem fundamentals.

High

High interventions will vary according to the reasons for the student's anger. Possible interventions are as follows:

1. If the student's anger is due to a crisis in personal life (birth of a sibling, divorce, serious illness or death in the family, etc.), teach coping skills, such as recognizing feelings of anger, control issues and depression; coming to terms with problems and learning to cope.
2. Teaching stress management skills may also be helpful.
3. If the student's anger is due to lack of social skills, teach communication skills, skills for making friends, and the like, as appropriate.
4. If the student's anger is due to deep-seated family or social problems, talk to your principal to see if some help is available.

Question 2

How many of the student's friends use alcohol or drugs?

Low

Interview the student for reasons, in order to select the appropriate intervention(s).

Suggestions for discussion topics include these: How much do your friends/acquaintances use drugs? Alcohol? When do you notice them using? How do you feel about their using? How many really close friends do you have? Does your closest friend use alcohol or other drugs? What kinds of things do you do with your friends? Why do you think kids use? What do you do in the afternoon. Is there anyone home when you get there? Where do you and your friends go? Have you or family members gone through any changes in the last year or two? (If so, how are you/family members managing?) Let student know it is normal to react to changes.

This initial interview may show you what additional interventions, if any, are needed.

Discovering what role the peers who drink or use drugs often play in the student's life will determine what level of intervention to implement. If a close friend or other important figures are substance abusers, high responses will almost surely be needed. If the student's relationship to substance-abusing peers is not very significant, medium responses may be sufficient.

Medium

Medium interventions may also include informal discussion and brain-storming of alternative behaviors, possibly with both teachers involved.

High

Provide opportunity for interaction with nonusing peers. Conduct a parent conference, if you suspect the student is using (or is at high risk for using) drugs. The conference may reveal a need for parent education.

Consider some of the following strategies:

1. Communicate with parents, agencies, or appropriate parties in order to inform them of the problem, determine the cause of the problem, and consider possible solutions to the problem.
2. Provide a drug information program if it is available.
3. Provide an orientation to penalties for the use of alcohol and drugs at school.
4. Involve the student in extracurricular activities as a redirection of interest.
5. Identify individuals the student may contact with his or her concerns (e.g., guidance counselor, school nurse, social worker, school psychologist, etc.).
6. Share concerns with the administration and seek referral to an agency for investigation of alcohol or drug abuse.

7. Encourage the student to become involved in athletic activities.
8. Assign the student activities which would require interactions with a respected role model (e.g., older student, high school student, college student, community leader, someone held in high esteem, etc.).
9. Provide the student with intelligent, accurate information concerning drugs and alcohol rather than sensationalized, scare tactic information.
10. Provide many opportunities for social and academic success.
11. Encourage the student to excel in a particular area of interest (e.g., provide information for him or her, provide personal and professional support, sponsor the student, etc.).
12. Provide the student with personal recognition during school hours (e.g., follow up on details of earlier communications, maintain a direction for conversation, etc.).
13. Lead and direct the student. Do not lecture and make demands.
14. Maintain anecdotal records of the student's behavior to check patterns or changes in behavior.
15. When natural consequences from peers occur as the result of the use of drugs or alcohol at school (e.g., criticism, loss of friendship, etc.), bring the consequences to the attention of the student.
16. Encourage the student's parents to be positive and helpful with the student as opposed to being negative and threatening.
17. Act as a resource for parents by providing information on agencies, counseling programs, and so on.
18. Teach the student to be satisfied with personal best effort rather than demanding perfection. Reduce the emphasis on competition and help the student realize that success is individually defined.
19. Be willing to take the time to listen, share, and talk with the student.
20. Listen to the student talk about his or her problems privately.
21. Increase your own professional knowledge of laws and treatment concerning drug and alcohol use and abuse.
22. Teach the student alternative ways to deal with demands, challenges, and pressures of the school-age experience (e.g., deal with problems when they arise, practice self-control at all times, share problems or concerns with others, etc.).
23. Maintain adequate supervision at all times and in all areas of the school (e.g., hallways, bathrooms, between classes, before and after school, etc.).

Question 3

How many close adults (relatives or friends) use alcohol or drugs frequently?

Low

Interview the student for reasons, in order to select the appropriate intervention(s).

Suggestions for discussion topics include these: How much do your friends/acquaintances use drugs? Alcohol? When do you notice them using? How do you feel about their using? How many really close friends do you have? Does your closest friend use alcohol or other drugs? What kinds of things do you do with your friends? Why do you think kids use? What do you do in the afternoon? Is there anyone home when you get there? Where do you and your friends go? Have you or family members gone through any changes in the last year or two? (If so, how are you/family members managing?) Let student know it is normal to react to changes.

This initial interview may show you what additional interventions, if any, are needed.

Discovering what role the peers who drink often play in the student's life will determine what level of intervention to implement. If a close friend or other important figures are substance abusers, high responses will almost surely be needed. If the student's relationship to substance abusing peers is not very significant, medium responses may be sufficient.

Medium

Medium interventions may also include informal discussion and brainstorming of alternative behaviors, possibly with both teachers involved.

High

Provide opportunity for interaction with nonusing peers. Conduct a parent conference, if you suspect the student is using (or is at high risk for using) drugs. The conference may reveal a need for parent education.

Consider some of the following strategies:

1. Communicate with parents, agencies, or appropriate parties in order to inform them of the problem, determine the cause of the problem, and consider possible solutions to the problem.
2. Provide a drug information program if it is available.
3. Provide an orientation to penalties for the use of alcohol and drugs at school.
4. Involve the student in extracurricular activities as a redirection of interest.
5. Identify individuals the student may contact with his or her concerns (e.g., guidance counselor, school nurse, social worker, school psychologist, etc.).
6. Share concerns with the administration and seek referral to an agency for investigation of alcohol or drug abuse.
7. Encourage the student to become involved in athletic activities.
8. Assign the student activities which would require interactions with a respected role model (e.g., older student, high school student, college student, community leader, someone held in high esteem, etc.).
9. Provide the student with intelligent, accurate information concerning drugs and alcohol rather than sensationalized, scare tactic information.
10. Provide many opportunities for social and academic success.
11. Encourage the student to excel in a particular area of interest (e.g., provide information for him or her, provide personal and professional support, sponsor the student, etc.).
12. Provide the student with personal recognition during school hours (e.g., follow up on details of earlier communications, maintain a direction for conversation, etc.).
13. Lead and direct the student. Do not lecture and make demands.
14. Maintain anecdotal records of the student's behavior to check patterns or changes in behavior.
15. When natural consequences from peers occur as the result of the use of drugs or alcohol at school (e.g., criticism, loss of friendship, etc.), bring the consequences to the attention of the student.
16. Encourage the student's parents to be positive and helpful with the student as opposed to being negative and threatening.

17. Act as a resource for parents by providing information on agencies, counseling programs, and so forth.

18. Teach the student to be satisfied with personal best effort rather than demanding perfection. Reduce the emphasis on competition and help the student realize that success is individually defined.

19. Be willing to take the time to listen, share, and talk with the student.

20. Listen to the student talk about his or her problems privately.

21. Increase your own professional knowledge of laws and treatment concerning drug and alcohol use and abuse.

22. Teach the student alternative ways to deal with demands, challenges, and pressures of the school-age experience (e.g., deal with problems when they arise, practice self-control at all times, share problems or concerns with others, etc.).

23. Maintain adequate supervision at all times and in all areas of the school (e.g., hallways, bathrooms, between classes, before and after school, etc.).

Question 4

How many times has the student been high or drunk?

Low

Interview the student for reasons, in order to select the appropriate intervention(s).

Suggestions for discussion topics include these: Tell me about your day. On what occasions do you drink? How often has that happened? Was the experience sufficiently enjoyable that he or she plans to repeat? How recent was this behavior? If this happened outside the home, how did the student get home? Boyfriend? Drunk driving? Invite the student to describe close friendships, what she or he does with friends, and so forth. If the student does have a problem, does she or he know it? Do the parents know? Has there already been some treatment, and if so, what were the results? The responses to these questions will guide you in your choice of additional interventions, if any.

Medium

Hold a parent conference, if indicated. If the student is behaving irresponsibly (i.e., drinking and driving), the parent needs to be informed. If the student is drinking or using drugs at all in grades 7–9, the parents should be informed. If older students have a problem the parents should be informed. If the student has been in some sort of treatment program, you might want to check the parents' perception of how successful it has been.

Provide drug and alcohol education for parents, if needed. Do parents need help with setting limits and communicating with adolescents, or education about the importance of parent involvement?

Assign the student to drug and alcohol education programs which provide information about the requirements of a healthy body, the physical and social effects of drug abuse, the symptoms of drug abuse, and learning to say no.

High

Give students opportunities to deal with personal issues. If the student's problem is related to a crisis in his or her personal life—divorce, serious illness, death in the family, and the like—teach coping skills such as recognizing feelings of anger, control issues, depression, coming to terms with problems, and learning to cope.

If the student may have a problem with substance abuse and no professional assessment has been done, discuss possible assistance with the principal.

Question 5

Is the student's family against drugs?

Low

Interview the student for reasons, in order to select the appropriate intervention(s).

Suggestions for discussion topics include the following: How much do your friends/acquaintances use drugs? Alcohol? When do you notice them using? How do you feel about their using? How many really close friends do you have? Does your closest friend use alcohol or other drugs? What kinds of things do you do with your friends? Why do you think kids use? What do you do in the afternoon. Is there anyone home when you get there? Where do you and your friends go? Have you or family members gone through any changes in the last year or two? (If so, how are you/ family members managing?) Let student know it is normal to react to changes.

This initial interview may show you what additional interventions, if any, are needed.

Discovering what role the peers who drink often play in the student's life will determine what level of intervention to implement. If close friend or other important figures are substance abusers, high responses will almost surely be needed. If the student's relationship to substance-abusing peers is not very significant, medium responses may be sufficient.

Medium

Medium interventions may also include informal discussion and brainstorming of alternative behaviors, possibly with both teachers involved.

High

Provide opportunity for interaction with nonusing peers. Conduct a parent conference, if you suspect the student is using (or is at high risk for using) drugs. The conference may reveal a need for parent education.

Consider some of the following strategies:

1. Communicate with parents, agencies, or appropriate parties to inform them of the problem, determine the cause of the problem, and consider possible solutions to the problem.
2. Provide a drug information program if it is available.
3. Provide an orientation to penalties for the use of alcohol and drugs at school.
4. Involve the student in extracurricular activities as a redirection of interest.
5. Identify individuals the student may contact with his or her concerns (e.g., guidance counselor, school nurse, social worker, school psychologist, etc.).

6. Share concerns with the administration and seek referral to an agency for investigation of alcohol or drug abuse.
7. Encourage the student to become involved in athletic activities.
8. Assign the student activities that would require interactions with a respected role model (e.g., older student, high school student, college student, community leader, someone held in high esteem, etc.).
9. Provide the student with intelligent, accurate information concerning drugs and alcohol rather than sensationalized, scare tactic information.
10. Provide many opportunities for social and academic success.
11. Encourage the student to excel in a particular area of interest (e.g., provide information for him or her, provide personal and professional support, sponsor the student, etc.).
12. Provide the student with personal recognition during school hours (e.g., follow up on details of earlier communications, maintain a direction for conversation, etc.).
13. Lead and direct the student. Do not lecture and make demands.
14. Maintain anecdotal records of the student's behavior to check patterns or changes in behavior.
15. When natural consequences from peers occur as the result of the use of drugs or alcohol at school (e.g., criticism, loss of friendship, etc.), bring the consequences to the attention of the student.
16. Encourage the student's parents to be positive and helpful with the student as opposed to being negative and threatening.
17. Act as a resource for parents by providing information on agencies, counseling programs, and so on.
18. Teach the student to be satisfied with personal best effort rather than demanding perfection. Reduce the emphasis on competition and help the student realize that success is individually defined.
19. Be willing to take the time to listen, share, and talk with the student.
20. Listen to the student talk about his or her problems privately.
21. Increase your own professional knowledge of laws and treatment concerning drug and alcohol use and abuse.
22. Teach the student alternative ways to deal with demands, challenges, and pressures of the school-age experience (e.g., deal with problems when they arise, practice self-control at all times, share problems or concerns with others, etc.).

23. Maintain adequate supervision at all times and in all areas of the school (e.g., hallways, bathrooms, between classes, before and after school, etc.).

Question 6

How often do the student's parents know where he or she is?

Low

Interview the student for reasons, to select the appropriate intervention(s).

First, establish a caring and helpful environment/relationship with the student so that the student will trust you to give you information.

You may share some information about yourself, that you care about students, that you experienced some challenging times growing up—whatever may be appropriate.

Topics for discussion may include these: If the student is in intermediate school, does the family have a child care problem? Have the parents indicated that they don't care where the student is? Is there evidence that they (parents) feel they can't control the student? What would happen if your [parents] did know what you are doing? Has your family gone through any major changes in the last few years? How do people in your family feel? What do people in your family think about? What would happen if something happened to you while you were out? How does your family feel about your friends? At what age do you think kids can take care of themselves? How do you know that? The responses will tell you what additional action, if any, is required.

Medium

Interview parents. The family may need referral to after-school programs.

If indicated by the information gathered in the interview, assign the student to a tutor who can provide ongoing support and monitoring of the student's situation. If your school does not have a tutoring program in place, this may be done informally. The tutor needs to have regularly scheduled contact with the student and provide "evidence" that there is someone who cares. This might involve helping with schoolwork or other problems, sending a birthday card and other little notes, and doing occasional activities together.

High

Discuss types of assistance available with your principal.

Lack of supervision may be so serious that a referral to child protective services is indicated because of neglect. Involve administrators and other appropriate and available personnel in this decision. If there is evidence for such a referral from your initial interview with the student, you need to proceed directly to this level of intervention after the interview.

Student may need close monitoring at school, having someone to "check in" with several times a day. The tutor would show care and concern in a benevolent manner.

Question 7

Would the student use drugs or alcohol if a friend dared him or her?

Low

Interview the student for reasons, to select the appropriate intervention(s).

First, establish a caring and helpful environment/relationship with the student so that the student will trust you to give you information.

You may share some information about yourself, that you care about students, that you experienced some challenging times growing up— whatever may be appropriate.

Topics for discussion may include, How many friends do you have? What do friends do together? What happens if a person does not have any friends? What does being a "friend" mean to you? Do you know what peer pressure is? How do most people handle peer pressure? Why do you think people have a hard time saying no? Does the student lack information about the dangers of drug use? Is the student attracted to drugs because of personal problems or a life crisis: Have you and/or your family gone through any big changes in the last few years? The responses will suggest what additional interventions, if any, are needed.

Medium

If indicated by the information gathered in the interview, assign the student to a tutor or counselor who can provide ongoing support and monitoring of the student's situation. If your school does not have a tutoring program in place, this may be done informally. The tutor needs to have regularly scheduled contact with the student and provide "evidence" that there is someone who cares. This might involve helping with schoolwork or other problems, sending a birthday card and other little notes, and doing occasional activities together.

Consider assigning the student to drug and alcohol education programs that provide information about the requirements of a healthy body, the physical and social effects of drug abuse, the symptoms of drug abuse, and learning to say no. Train the student in refusal and assertiveness skills beyond those offered in standard drug education programs.

High

If the student's response is that he or she would "try it," proceed with all of the interventions suggested already, and consider these additional responses:

Conduct a parent conference, if you suspect the student already is (or may soon become) involved with drugs. The conference may reveal a need for parent education programs. Do parents need help with setting limits and communicating with adolescents, education about the importance of parent involvement, and so forth.

If the student is experiencing a life crisis, consider teaching skills for coping: recognizing feelings of anger, control issues and depression; coming to terms with problems and learning to cope.

Question 8

How many times has the student been arrested?

Low

Interview the student for reasons, to select the appropriate intervention(s).

First, establish a caring and helpful environment/relationship with the student so that the student will trust you to give you information.

You may share some information about yourself, that you care about students, that you experienced some challenging times growing up—whatever may be appropriate.

Topics for discussion may include these: What happens during your day/after school/evenings/weekends? Have your and/or your family gone through any big changes in the last few years? What kinds of things make you angry? How do people usually express anger? What happens to them? How are you doing in class? What do you think about your teacher? What does your teacher think about you? What subject(s) do you like/not like? What consequences do you have at school/home for being arrested? How many arrests have their been? For what reasons? How long ago? What were the results? Is the student on probation? How do family and student feel about the situation? Do academic and/or personal problems play a role? The answers to these questions will help you to select interventions. (Students who have been arrested are often poorly bonded to social institutions like school. In addition, many have experienced lack of success in school, which decreases bonding.)

Medium

If indicated by the information gathered in the interview, assign the student to a tutor who can provide ongoing support and monitoring of the student's situation. If your school does not have a tutoring program in place, this may be done informally. The tutor needs to have regularly scheduled contact with the student and provide "evidence" that there is someone who cares. This might involve help with schoolwork or other problems, written communication, and occasional activities together.

Assign a peer adviser. If the arrests may be partially a function of poor choice of friends and your school offers peer advisors or a similar program, refer student to that program.

Provide needed academic assistance. This might include tutoring or ESL.

Hold a parent conference. Do parents need help with setting limits and communicating with adolescents, or education about the importance of parent involvement?

Consult with other school personnel, such as counselors and administrators. Is everyone who should be aware of the student's history? Has there been contact with a parole officer, social worker, or any outside social agency? If not, does the school wish to initiate contact?

High

Contact the student's probation officer and social worker. If the student is currently actively involved with the courts, he or she may well have a probation officer and/or social worker. Sometimes it is possible for all agencies involved with a student to work with the school on helping the student.

Deal with personal problems. If the student's problem is related to a crisis in her personal life—divorce, serious illness, or death in the family—teach coping skills, such as recognizing feelings of anger, control issues, depression, coming to terms with problems, and learning to cope.

Consider referral for individual and/or group counseling for the student and family counseling within the district/city/county, if the student's behavior is due to deep-seated family or social problems.

Question 9

Has the student ever been suspended or expelled?

Low

Interview the student for reasons, to select the appropriate intervention(s).

First, establish a caring and helpful environment/relationship with the student so that the student will trust you to give you information.

You may share some information about yourself, that you care about students, that you experienced some challenging times growing up—whatever may be appropriate.

Topics for discussion may include the following: What do you think of/feel about school? What happened to cause you to be suspended? How are things at home? When did things get tough here at school? How are your relationships going (friends, family, etc.)? Is there anything you feel really angry about now? Have you or your family members been through any big changes in the last few years? This year? (Check file.) How many times have you been suspended? What happens at home when this occurs? The student's response will guide you in deciding which additional interventions, if any, are needed.

Medium

See if you can help with schoolwork or other problems, sending a birthday card and other little notes, and doing occasional activities together.

Hold a parent conference. Explore the same topics you covered in the interview with the student. In addition, does parent appear to need help with parenting skills and/or training in how to help a child with behavior/anger management? You may be able to do this parent education during the conference.

High

If indicated, talk to the principal about instruction in social skills if student's misbehavior reflects lack of knowledge in interpersonal communication and/or lack of social skills. Discuss understanding ones own personality style, making friends, being a friend, communicating needs, and so forth. If the student is experiencing a life crisis, consider teaching skills for coping: recognizing feelings of anger, control issues, and depression; coming to terms with problems and learning to cope.

Question 10

How many D's and F's did the student get on the last report card?

Low

Interview the student for reasons, to select the appropriate intervention(s).

First, establish a caring and helpful environment/relationship with the student so that the student will trust you to give you information.

You may share some information about yourself, that you care about students, that you experienced some challenging times growing up—whatever may be appropriate.

Topics for discussion may include, What do you think of/feel about school? What do you think of your teacher? What is your favorite subject? Least favorite? Tell me what happens after school/evenings/weekends. Have you and/or your family gone through any big changes? Who do you hang around with at school? What is the hardest thing about school? Is there anyone to help you at home? What year in school was your best/most difficult? (You may need to check file, especially for younger students.) Is there a language or other learning difficulty? Responses to these questions will identify what, if any, interventions may be helpful.

Medium

See if you can help with schoolwork or other problems, send a birthday card and other little notes, and do occasional activities together.

Parent conference. Explore the same topics you covered in the interview with the student. In addition, does parent appear to need help with parenting skills and/or training in how to help a child with schoolwork? You may be able to do this parent education during the conference.

Consider using a behavior modification program with the student, such as a daily contract for getting work done on time and correctly, with an appropriate system of positive responses.

High

If there appear to be severe academic problems, see if they seem to be a function of personal problems. If the student is experiencing a life crisis, consider teaching skills for coping: recognizing feelings of anger, control issues, and depression; coming to terms with problems and learning to cope.

Question 11

Does the student have a juvenile delinquency record?

Low

Interview the student for reasons, to select the appropriate intervention(s).

First, establish a caring and helpful environment/relationship with the student so that the student will trust you to give you information.

You may share some information about yourself, that you care about students, that you experienced some challenging times growing up — whatever may be appropriate.

Topics for discussion may include, What do you think of/feel about school? What happened that you have a record? What was your best year in school? The toughest year? Have you/your family been through any big changes in the last few years? This year? How do people in your family handle anger? What happens when people feel angry? How do people usually show anger? How did your family respond to your record? How are things now?

Do academic and/or personal problems play a role? The answers to these questions will help you to select a response. (Students who have records are often poorly bonded to social institutions like school. In addition, many have experienced lack of success in school, which decreases bonding, as well.)

Medium

Assign a tutor to monitor student's progress and provide opportunity to increase the student's bonding to the school. If your school does not have a tutoring program in place, this could be done informally. The tutor needs to have regularly scheduled contact with the student and to provide "evidence" that there is someone who cares. This might involve written communication, help with schoolwork or other problems, and occasional activities together.

Assign a peer adviser. If the record may be partially a function of poor choice of friends, and your school offers peer advisers or a similar program, refer student to that program.

Provide needed academic assistance. This might include tutoring or ESL.

Hold a parent conference. If appropriate, discuss how things are going now with the student. Do parents need help with setting limits and communicating with adolescents, or education about the importance of parent involvement?

Consult with other school personnel, such as counselors and adminis-trators. Is everyone who should be aware of the student's history? Has there been contact with a parole officer, social worker or any outside so-cial agency? If not, does the school wish to initiate contact?

High

Contact the student's probation officer and social worker. If the student is currently actively involved with the courts, he or she may well have a pro-bation officer and/or social worker. Sometimes it is possible for all agencies involved with a student to work with the school on helping the student.

Deal with personal problems. You may need to refer the student to an outside agency. If the student's problem is related to a crisis in her per-sonal life (e.g., divorce, serious illness, or death in the family, etc.), teach coping skills, such as recognizing feelings of anger, control issues, and de-pression; coming to terms with problems, and learning to cope.

Question 12

Does the student have a certifiable disability?

Low

Interview the student for reasons, to select the appropriate intervention(s).

First, establish a caring and helpful environment/relationship with the student so that the student will trust you to give you information.

You may share some information about yourself, that you care about students, that you experienced some challenging times growing up—whatever may be appropriate.

Topics for discussion may include these: What do you think of/feel about school? What is the nature of the disability? If treatment is needed, is the student getting it? Does family need help in locating resources? Does the disability cause problems with academic activities and/or with peers? If so, are these problems being appropriately addressed? What attitudes do student and family have toward the disability? The answers to these ques-tions will help you to select additional interventions, if any are needed.

Medium

Refer student to appropriate health care or other experts if additional treatment or diagnosis is needed.

Arrange for appropriate support, if needed. This might be academic help, such as tutoring. It might be special services, such as speech therapy or physical therapy, or the services of the specialist for the visually impaired. It might be the provision of special resources—large-print books for a visually impaired student, for example. Consult with district special education personnel if you are unsure about what resources and programs might be appropriate and available.

Hold a parent conference, if indicated. The subject will be a function of what you have learned about the student and what you want to do to help. Parents may be unaware of available resources, for example, or, on the other hand, they may be able to make you aware of new resources and additional information about the student and his problem. If the student is having problems with acceptance and self-image, this may need to be addressed.

High

Refer student and/or family for counseling with special education staff, if needed. Sometimes families need expert help in coming to terms with a disability.

Question 13

How many times was the student absent last semester?

Low

Interview the student for reasons, to select the appropriate intervention(s).

First, establish a caring and helpful environment/relationship with the student so that the student will trust you to give you information.

You may share some information about yourself, that you care about students, that you experienced some challenging times growing up—whatever may be appropriate.

Topics for discussion may include the following: What kinds of things keep you at home? (Check file or other records for a pattern of excessive absences.) What do you think of school this year? What do you like/dislike. Tell me about your friends. What do you think of your teachers this year? What do your teachers think about you? Have you or family members been through any big changes (new baby, financial, divorce, loss, moving, etc.)? What happens when you get sick? Who takes care of you? (Does the student have a neglected or undetected health problem? If indicated, consider additional interventions, working with your school nurse or community health programs.) How are things at home? (Check for any signs of abuse, and make appropriate reports to your school team and child protective services.) Responses in this interview will direct you to other interventions, if any.

Medium

Monitor student absence. Consider a behavior modification program to improve attendance—some schools have special attendance clubs; individual teachers can also design a program of attendance incentives.

Assign student to a tutor, to increase student's bonding to school—many students are convinced that "nobody cares whether I'm here or not. They probably don't even notice." If indicated by the information gathered in the interview, assign the student to a tutor or counselor who can provide ongoing support and monitoring of the student's situation. If your school does not have a tutoring program in place, this may be done informally. The tutor needs to have regularly scheduled contact with the student and provide "evidence" that there is someone who cares. This might involve help with schoolwork or other problems, sending a birthday card and other little notes, and occasional activities together.

Refer student or family to school nurse or outside health provider, if student has (or may have) unmet health needs.

If the behaviors seem to be a cry for attention, consider assigning a student "special friend" to give the student recognition and extra attention.

High

If student is absent due to parental neglect, babysitting, or other reason, hold a parent conference, possible referral to district or site attendance personnel, and/or SARB [student attendance review board], report to child protective services or other appropriate agency.

If absences seem related to emotional problems, consider referral for counseling. If student is experiencing a life crisis—serious illness or death in the family, divorce, birth of a sibling, or the like—consider teaching skills for coping. This includes learning to recognize feelings of anger, control issues, and depression; learning to come to terms with problems and learning to cope.

Question 14

Did the student move or change schools last year?

Low

Interview the student for reasons, to select the appropriate intervention(s).

First, establish a caring and helpful environment/relationship with the student so that the student will trust you to give you information.

You may share some information about yourself, that you care about students, that you experienced some challenging times growing up—whatever may be appropriate.

Topics for discussion may include the following: Sometimes it's hard for people to move. What is moving like for you? Which move did you like? What was the hardest move? A lot of people have a hard time making new friends. How have you done with making friends? What do you like to do with your friends? What kind of things do friends like to do here at this school? How are things going at home? What do you think of school/your teacher? Have you or other family members been through other big changes in the last year? When there are lots of changes it is sometimes hard on families. How are you doing? How is your workload here at school? How long do you spend on homework? The student's responses will determine the interventions you select, if any.

Medium

If indicated by the or information gathered in the interview, assign the student to a tutor who can provide ongoing support and monitoring of the student's situation. If your school does not have a tutoring program in place, this may be done informally. The tutor needs to have regularly scheduled contact with the student and provide "evidence" that there is someone who cares. This might involve help with schoolwork or other problems, sending a birthday card and other little notes, and doing occasional activities together.

Medium interventions may also include informal discussion and brainstorming of alternative behaviors and teaching of social skills or self-esteem fundamentals.

It may also be helpful to assign a "special friend" to the student. Make use of your contact with and knowledge of the other students to find students who would enjoy doing this and who would also be in contact with you or other tutors, so that the peer does not feel responsible for the student's behavior.

High

If the student has been through family changes and is feeling sad, she or he may not understand this natural emotion. The need may be in the area of social skills.

Individual or group counseling programs may help this student to talk with others who have been through changes and learn coping skills.

If the student seems angry or depressed, talk to the principal about referral of student to school/community counseling services. Family referral to outside agencies may also be helpful.

Appendix C

Elementary Risk Assessment

Please select the questions you wish to use, copy them one by one, and make a list of them for students to use as a questionnaire.

Question 1

How often is the student angry?

Low

Interview the student for reasons, in order to select the appropriate intervention(s).

First, establish a caring and helpful environment/relationship with the student so that the student will trust you to give you information.

You may share some information about yourself, that you care about students, that you experienced some challenging times growing up (whatever may be appropriate).

Suggestions for discussion topics include the following: Tell me about your day. Is there a particular time of the day you notice anger? Is there a particular situation/person (teacher, peer, parent, important relationship, etc.) that triggers anger for you? Have you gone through any family or relationship changes in the last few years?

This initial interview may show you what additional interventions, if any, are needed. For example, if student's anger is a result of inadequate social skills, identifying and teaching particular skills may be helpful. If the anger is due to a family crisis, other responses will be more appropriate (see examples later).

Medium

If indicated by information gathered in the interview, work with another teacher to provide ongoing support and monitoring of the student's situation. This might involve help with schoolwork or other problems, sending a birthday card and other little notes, and occasional activities together.

Medium interventions may also include informal discussion and brainstorming of alternative behaviors and teaching of social skills or self-esteem fundamentals.

High

High interventions will vary according to the reasons for the student's anger. Possible interventions are as follows:

1. If the student's anger is due to a crisis in his or her personal life—birth of a sibling, divorce, serious illness or death in the family, etc.—teach coping skills, such as recognizing feelings of anger, control issues and depression; coming to terms with problems and learning to cope.
2. Teaching stress management skills may also be helpful.
3. If the student's anger is due to lack of social skills, teach communication skills, skills for making friends, and so forth, as appropriate.
4. If the student's anger is due to deep-seated family or social problems, talk to your principal to see if some help is available.

Question 2

How many close adults (relatives or friends) use alcohol frequently?

Low

Interview the student for reasons, in order to select the appropriate intervention(s).

Suggestions for discussion topics include the following: How much do your friends/acquaintances use drugs? Alcohol? When do you notice them using? How do you feel about their using? How many really close friends do you have? Does your closest friend use alcohol or other drugs? What kinds of things do you do with your friends? Why do you think kids use? What do you do in the afternoon? Is there anyone home when you get there? Where do you and your friends go? Have you or family members gone through any changes in the last year or two? (If so, how are you/family managing?) Let student know it is normal to react to changes.

This initial interview may show you what additional interventions, if any, are needed.

Discovering what role the peers who drink often play in the student's life will determine what level of intervention to implement. If a close friend or other important figures are substance abusers, high responses will almost surely be needed. If the student's relationship to substance abusing peers is not very significant, medium responses may be sufficient.

Medium

Medium interventions may also include informal discussion and brainstorming of alternative behaviors, possibly with both teachers involved.

High

Provide opportunity for interaction with nonusing peers. Conduct a parent conference if you suspect the student is using (or is at high risk for using) drugs. The conference may reveal a need for parent education.

Consider some of the following strategies:

1. Communicate with parents, agencies, or appropriate parties in order to inform them of the problem, determine the cause of the problem, and consider possible solutions to the problem.
2. Provide a drug information program if it is available.
3. Provide an orientation to penalties for the use of alcohol and drugs at school.
4. Involve the student in extracurricular activities as a redirection of interest.

5. Identify individuals the student may contact with his or her concerns (e.g., guidance counselor, school nurse, social worker, school psychologist, etc.).

6. Share concerns with the administration and seek referral to an agency for investigation of alcohol or drug abuse.

7. Encourage the student to become involved in athletic activities.

8. Assign the student activities which would require interactions with a respected role model (e.g., older student, high school student, college student, community leader, someone held in high esteem, etc.).

9. Provide the student with intelligent, accurate information concerning drugs and alcohol rather than sensationalized, scare tactic information.

10. Provide many opportunities for social and academic success.

11. Encourage the student to excel in a particular area of interest (e.g., provide information for him/her, provide personal and professional support, sponsor the student, etc.).

12. Provide the student with personal recognition during school hours (e.g., follow up on details of earlier communications, maintain a direction for conversation, etc.).

13. Lead and direct the student. Do not lecture and make demands.

14. Maintain anecdotal records of the student's behavior to check patterns or changes in behavior.

15. When natural consequences from peers occur as the result of the use of drugs or alcohol at school (e.g., criticism, loss of friendship, etc.), bring the consequences to the attention of the student.

16. Encourage the student's parents to be positive and helpful with the student as opposed to being negative and threatening.

17. Act as a resource for parents by providing information on agencies, counseling programs, and so forth.

18. Teach the student to be satisfied with personal best effort rather than demanding perfection. Reduce the emphasis on competition and help the student realize that success is individually defined.

19. Be willing to take the time to listen, share, and talk with the student.

20. Listen to the student talk about his or her problems privately.

21. Increase your own professional knowledge of laws and treatment concerning drug and alcohol use and abuse.

22. Teach the student alternative ways to deal with demands, challenges, and pressures of the school-age experience (e.g., deal with

problems when they arise, practice self-control at all times, share problems or concerns with others, etc.).

23. Maintain adequate supervision at all times and in all areas of the school (e.g., hallways, bathrooms, between classes, before and after school, etc.).

Question 3

Is the student afraid to express anger?

Low

Interview the student for reasons, in order to select the appropriate intervention(s).

First, establish a caring and helpful environment/relationship with the student so that the student will trust you to give you information.

You may share some information about yourself, that you care about students, that you experienced some challenging times growing up (whatever may be appropriate).

Suggestions for discussion topics include the following: Tell me about your day. Is there a particular time of the day you notice anger? Is there a particular situation/person (teacher, peer, parent, important relationship, etc.) that triggers anger for you? Have you gone through any family or relationship changes in the last few years?

This initial interview may show you what additional interventions, if any, are needed. For example, if student's anger is a result of inadequate social skills, identifying and teaching particular skills may be helpful. If the anger is due to a family crisis, other responses will be more appropriate (see examples later).

Medium

Try to find time to help the student with schoolwork or other problems, sending a birthday card and other little notes, and occasional activities together.

Medium interventions may also include informal discussion and brainstorming of alternative behaviors and teaching of social skills or self-esteem fundamentals.

High

High interventions will vary according to the reasons for the student's anger. Possible interventions are as follows:

1. If the student's anger is due to a crisis in his or her personal life— birth of a sibling, divorce, serious illness or death in the family, etc.—teach coping skills, such as recognizing feelings of anger, control issues and depression; coming to terms with problems and learning to cope.
2. Teaching stress management skills may also be helpful.
3. If the student's anger is due to lack of social skills, teach communication skills, skills for making friends, and so forth, as appropriate.
4. If the student's anger is due to deep-seated family or social problems, ask the principal for help in finding assistance for the student.

Question 4

Is the student's family against drugs?

Low

Interview the student for reasons, to select the appropriate intervention(s).

Suggestions for discussion topics include the following: How much do your friends/acquaintances use drugs? Alcohol? When do you notice them using? How do you feel about their using? How many really close friends do you have? Does your closest friend use alcohol or other drugs? What kinds of things do you do with your friends? Why do you think kids use? What do you do in the afternoon? Is there anyone home when you get there? Where do you and your friends go? Have you or family members gone through any changes in the last year or two? (If so, how are you/family managing?) Let student know it is normal to react to changes.

This initial interview may show you what additional interventions, if any, are needed.

Discovering what role the peers who drink often play in the student's life will determine what level of intervention to implement. If close friends or other important figures are substance abusers, high responses will almost surely be needed. If the student's relationship to substance abusing peers is not very significant, medium responses may be sufficient.

Medium

Medium interventions may also include informal discussion and brainstorming of alternative behaviors, possibly with both teachers involved.

High

Provide opportunity for interaction with nonusing peers. Conduct a parent conference if you suspect the student is using (or is at high risk for using) drugs. The conference may reveal a need for parent education.

Consider some of the following strategies:

1. Communicate with parents, agencies, or appropriate parties in order to inform them of the problem, determine the cause of the problem, and consider possible solutions to the problem.
2. Provide a drug information program if it is available.
3. Provide an orientation to penalties for the use of alcohol and drugs at school.
4. Involve the student in extracurricular activities as a redirection of interest.
5. Identify individuals the student may contact with his or her concerns (e.g., guidance counselor, school nurse, social worker, school psychologist, etc.).
6. Share concerns with the administration and seek referral to an agency for investigation of alcohol or drug abuse.
7. Encourage the student to become involved in athletic activities.
8. Assign the student activities which would require interactions with a respected role model (e.g., older student, high school student, college student, community leader, someone held in high esteem, etc.).
9. Provide the student with intelligent, accurate information concerning drugs and alcohol rather than sensationalized, scare tactic information.

10. Provide many opportunities for social and academic success.

11. Encourage the student to excel in a particular area of interest (e.g., provide information for him or her, provide personal and professional support, sponsor the student, etc.).

12. Provide the student with personal recognition during school hours (e.g., follow up on details of earlier communications, maintain a direction for conversation, etc.).

13. Lead and direct the student. Do not lecture and make demands.

14. Maintain anecdotal records of the student's behavior to check patterns or changes in behavior.

15. When natural consequences from peers occur as the result of the use of drugs or alcohol at school (e.g., criticism, loss of friendship, etc.), bring the consequences to the attention of the student.

16. Encourage the student's parents to be positive and helpful with the student as opposed to being negative and threatening.

17. Act as a resource for parents by providing information on agencies, counseling programs, and so forth.

18. Teach the student to be satisfied with personal best effort rather than demanding perfection. Reduce the emphasis on competition and help the student realize that success is individually defined.

19. Be willing to take the time to listen, share, and talk with the student.

20. Listen to the student talk about his or her problems privately.

21. Increase your own professional knowledge of laws and treatment concerning drug and alcohol use and abuse.

22. Teach the student alternative ways to deal with demands, challenges, and pressures of the school-age experience (e.g., deal with problems when they arise, practice self-control at all times, share problems or concerns with others, etc.).

23. Maintain adequate supervision at all times and in all areas of the school (e.g., hallways, bathrooms, between classes, before and after school, etc.).

Question 5

How often do the student's parents know where he or she is?

Low

Interview the student for reasons, in order to select the appropriate intervention(s).

First, establish a caring and helpful environment/relationship with the student so that the student will trust you to give you information.

You may share some information about yourself, that you care about students, that you experienced some challenging times growing up (whatever may be appropriate).

Topics for discussion may include the following: Does the family have a child care problem? Have the parents indicated that they don't care where the student is? Is there evidence that the parents feel they can't control the student? What would happen if your parents did know what you are doing? Has your family gone through any major changes in the last few years? How do people in your family feel? What do people in your family think about? What would happen if something happened to you while you were out? How does your family feel about your friends? At what age do you think kids can take care of themselves? How do you know that? The responses will tell you what additional action, if any, is required.

Medium

Interview parents. The family should understand that students need to know that their parents care about them and want to know where they are after school, a time when students often get into various kinds of trouble. A top predictor of drug use among students is "their parents don't know where they are after school."

High

Lack of supervision may be so serious that you need to involve administrators and other appropriate and available personnel in this decision. If there is evidence for such a referral from your initial interview with the student, you should proceed directly to this level of intervention after the interview.

Student may need close monitoring at school, having someone to "check in" with several times a day. Show care and concern in a benevolent manner.

Question 6

Does the student often feel all alone?

Low

Interview the student for reasons, in order to select the appropriate intervention(s).

First, establish a caring and helpful environment/relationship with the student so that the student will trust you to give you information.

You may share some information about yourself, that you care about students, that you experienced some challenging times growing up (whatever may be appropriate).

Topics for discussion may include the following: Tell me about your day. Is the student lonely due to problems making friends? If that is the problem, is it shyness, being new, or the fact that something about the student's behavior causes peers to reject him or her? Has your family gone through any changes in the last few years? How does it feel for you to be alone? What do you think about? What happens when you get home from school? What do you and your family do after school/in the evening/on the weekend? What kinds of things make people sad? What happens when people feel sad? Choose appropriate medium and/or high interventions according to the results of this interview.

Medium

You might help with schoolwork or other problems, send a birthday card and other little notes, and have occasional activities together.

It may also be helpful to assign a "special friend" to the student. Make use of your contact with and knowledge of the other students to find students who would enjoy doing this and who would also be in contact with you or other mentors, so that the peer does not feel responsible for the identified student's behavior.

High

If the student has been through family changes and is feeling sad, he or she may not understand this natural emotion. See if you can help the student learn assertive social skills to reach out to peers.

If the student seems depressed, talk to the principal about possible assistance.

Question 7

Do the student's parents/guardians listen and understand the student?

Low

Interview the student for reasons, in order to select the appropriate intervention(s).

First, establish a caring and helpful environment/relationship with the student so that the student will trust you to give you information.

You may share some information about yourself, that you care about students, that you experienced some challenging times growing up (whatever may be appropriate).

Topics for discussion may include the following: Whom do you share your thoughts and feelings with at school/home? What happens when you get home from school/in the evening/weekends? When do people in your family talk? What happens when people in your family talk together? How do you feel during the day? Check to see if parents' hectic work scheduling makes it difficult to provide support. Has your family been through any big changes in the last few years? Is there evidence that parents are unaware of the importance of listening to their children? The student's response to these questions will suggest what level of intervention would be beneficial, if any.

Medium

It may be helpful to conduct a parent conference. The content will be a function of the results of the student interview and the responses the parent makes during this conference. It may be that the family is experiencing a crisis or has many demands and needs referral to outside agencies. The parent may need/desire parent education. This education may simply take the form of the communication that occurs at this conference—the parent becomes aware of the student's feelings and understands the significance of his or her responsiveness

Teaching the student social skills to express thoughts and feelings may be beneficial. Modeling sharing and teaching social conversation and listening skills may be needed.

High

The student may be experiencing some kind of life crisis—birth of a sibling, serious illness or death of a family member or other significant person, family financial crisis, divorce, and the like. If so, provide support and instruction in coping skills, such as recognizing feelings of anger, control issues and depression; coming to terms with problems and learning to cope.

Ask the principal for suggestions of resources that could help the student and his or her family.

Question 8

Has the student ever been sent to the principal?

Low

Interview the student for reasons, in order to select the appropriate intervention(s).

First, establish a caring and helpful environment/relationship with the student so that the student will trust you to give you information.

You may share some information about yourself, that you care about students, that you experienced some challenging times growing up (whatever may be appropriate).

Topics for discussion may include the following: How many times have you been sent to the principal's office? What is your version of what happened (choose one or more occasions)?

Tell me about the kids at school. What happens during your day/after school/evenings/weekends? Have your and/or your family gone through any big changes in the last few years? What kinds of things make you angry? How do people usually express anger? What happens to them? How are you doing in class? What do you think about your teacher? What does your teacher think about you? What subject(s) do you like/not like? What consequences do you have at school/home for seeing the principal?

The responses will guide your choice of any additional interventions.

Medium

Consider a behavior modification program focused on reducing the number of incidents of misbehavior and/or referrals, rewarding the student for appropriate behavior, etc.

Hold a parent conference. Is behavior the same at home? If not, what does the parent think is wrong at school? If behavior is the same at home, offer help.

Provide new responsibilities as alternative activities to replace the patterns that have gotten the student into trouble. Provide opportunities for involvement in clubs, scouts, and other activities. Give the student a special responsibility (something active) at school, and recognition for completion.

Provide academic assistance, if behavior problems are related to academic problems. (Sample programs may include tutoring, peer tutoring, ESL, changing student's program, referral to the student study team, or help for parents on how to work with the child at home.)

High

Provide instruction in social skills, if student's misbehavior reflects lack of knowledge in interpersonal communication and or lack of social skills that lead to aggressive responses. Consider special instruction in these areas: understanding his or her own personality style, making friends, being a friend, communicating needs, etc.

If the behaviors seem connected to a lack of interpersonal skills and relationships with peers, consider assigning a student "special friend" to give the student recognition and extra attention.

Monitor frequency and severity of referrals to the principal, to see if problems persist.

Question 9

How many D's and F's did the student get on the last report card?

Low

Interview the student for reasons, in order to select the appropriate intervention(s).

First, establish a caring and helpful environment/relationship with the student so that the student will trust you to give you information.

You may share some information about yourself, that you care about students, that you experienced some challenging times growing up (whatever may be appropriate).

Topics for discussion may include the following: What do you think of/feel about school? What do you think of your teacher? What is your favorite subject? Least favorite? Tell me what happens after school/evenings/weekends. Have you and/or your family gone through any big changes? Who do you hang around with at school? What is the hardest thing about school? Is there anyone to help you at home? What year in school was your best/most difficult? (You may need to check cummulative file, especially for younger students.) Is there a language or other learning difficulty? Responses to these questions will identify what, if any, interventions may be helpful.

Medium

See if you can help with schoolwork or other problems, sending a birthday card and other little notes, and occasional activities together.

Hold a parent conference. Explore the same topics you covered in the interview with the student. In addition, does parent appear to need help with parenting skills and/or training in how to help a child with schoolwork? You may be able to do this parent education during the conference.

Consider using a behavior modification program with the student, such as a daily contract for getting work done on time and correctly, with an appropriate system of positive responses.

High

If there appear to be severe academic problems, see if they seem to be a function of personal problems. If the student is experiencing a life crisis, consider teaching skills for coping: recognizing feelings of anger, control issues and depression; coming to terms with problems and learning to cope.

Question 10

Has the student ever been suspended or expelled?

Low

Interview the student for reasons, in order to select the appropriate intervention(s).

First, establish a caring and helpful environment/relationship with the student so that the student will trust you to give you information.

You may share some information about yourself, that you care about students, that you experienced some challenging times growing up (whatever may be appropriate).

Topics for discussion may include the following: What do you think of/feel about school? What happened to cause you to be suspended/expelled? How are things at home? When did things get tough here at school? How are your relationships going (friends, family, etc.)? Anything you feel really angry about now? Have you or your family members been through any big changes in the last few years? This year? (Check file.) How many times have you been suspended? What happens at home when this occurs? The student's response will guide you in deciding which additional interventions, if any, are needed.

Medium

See if you can help with schoolwork or other problems, sending a birthday card and other little notes, and occasional activities together.

Hold a parent conference. Explore the same topics you covered in the interview with the student. In addition, does the parent appear to need help with parenting skills and/or training in how to help a child with behavior/

anger management and other skills? You may be able to do this parent education during the conference.

High

If indicated, talk to the principal about instruction in social skills if student's misbehavior reflects lack of knowledge in interpersonal communication and/or lack of social skills. Discuss understanding one's own personality style, making friends, being a friend, communicating needs, and so forth. If the student is experiencing a life crisis, consider teaching skills for coping: recognizing feelings of anger, control issues and depression; coming to terms with problems and learning to cope.

Question 11

How many times was the student absent last semester?

Low

Interview the student for reasons, in order to select the appropriate intervention(s).

First, establish a caring and helpful environment/relationship with the student so that the student will trust you to give you information.

You may share some information about yourself, that you care about students, that you experienced some challenging times growing up (whatever may be appropriate).

Topics for discussion may include the following: What kinds of things keep you at home? (Check file or other records for a pattern of excessive absences.) What do you think of school this year? What do you like/dislike? Tell me about your friends. What do you think of your teacher this year? What does your teacher think about you? Have you or family members been through any big changes (new baby, financial, divorce, loss, moving, etc.)? What happens when you get sick? Who takes care of you? (Does the student have a neglected or undetected health problem? If indicated, consider additional interventions, working with your school nurse or community health programs.) How are things at home? (Check for any signs of abuse, and make appropriate reports to your school team and child protective services.) Responses in this interview will direct you to other interventions, if any.

Medium

Monitor student absence. Consider a behavior modification program to improve attendance—some schools have special attendance clubs; individual teachers can also design a program of attendance incentives.

Assign student to a tutor, to increase student's bonding to school— many students are convinced that "nobody cares whether I'm here or not. They probably don't even notice." If indicated by information gathered in the interview, assign the student to a tutor who can provide ongoing support and monitoring of the student's situation. If your school does not have a tutoring program in place, this may be done informally. The tutor needs to have regularly scheduled contact with the student and provide "evidence" that there is someone who cares. This might involve help with schoolwork or other problems, sending a birthday card and other little notes, and occasional activities together.

Refer student or family to school nurse or outside health provider, if student has (or may have) unmet health needs.

If the behaviors seem to be a cry for attention, consider assigning a student "special friend" to give the student recognition and extra attention.

If the student indicates that he or she was absent for reasons other than illness or for very minor complaints, the following interventions are recommended:

High

If student absence is due to parental neglect, babysitting, etc., hold a parent conference, possible referral to district or site attendance personnel, and/or SARB [student attendance review board], report to child protective services, etc.

If absences seem related to emotional problems, consider referral for counseling. If student is experiencing a life crisis (serious illness or death in the family, divorce, birth of a sibling, etc.), consider teaching skills for coping. This includes learning to recognize feelings of anger, control issues, and depression; learning to come to terms with problems and learning to cope.

Question 12

How many times did the student move or change schools last year?

Low

Interview the student for reasons, in order to select the appropriate intervention(s).

First, establish a caring and helpful environment/relationship with the student so that the student will trust you to give you information.

You may share some information about yourself, that you care about students, that you experienced some challenging times growing up (whatever may be appropriate).

Topics for discussion may include the following: Sometimes it's hard for people to move. What is moving like for you? Which move did you like? What was the hardest move? A lot of people have a hard time making new friends. How have you done with making friends? What do you like to do with your friends? What kind of things do friends like to do here at this school? How are things going at home? What do you think of school/your teacher? Have you or other family members been through other big changes in the last year? When there are lots of changes it is sometimes hard on families. How are you doing? How is your workload here at school? How long do you spend on homework? The student's responses will determine the interventions you select, if any.

Medium

If indicated by the information gathered in the interview, assign the student to a tutor who can provide ongoing support and monitoring of the student's situation. If your school does not have a mentoring program in place, this may be done informally. The tutor needs to have regularly scheduled contact with the student and provide "evidence" that there is someone who cares. This might involve help with schoolwork or other problems, sending a birthday card and other little notes, and occasional activities together.

Medium interventions may also include informal discussion and brainstorming of alternative behaviors and teaching of social skills or self-esteem fundamentals.

It may also be helpful to assign a "special friend" to the student. Make use of your contact with and knowledge of the other students to find students who would enjoy doing this and who would also be in contact with you or other mentors, so that the peer does not feel responsible for the student's behavior.

High

If the student has been through family changes and is feeling sad, he or she may not understand this natural emotion. The need may be in the area of social skills.

Individual or group counseling programs may help this student to talk with others who have been through changes and learn coping skills.

If the student seems angry or depressed, talk to the principal about referral of student to school/community counseling services. Family referral to outside agencies may also be helpful.

GUIDELINES FOR INTERPRETING THE RESULTS OF THE RISK ASSESSMENT

1. The interventions suggested are in order of intensity, *low* requiring the least intensive intervention, and *high* the most intensive.
2. You as the teacher can often provide most low responses as a part of your usual and expected interactions with students and parents. Medium responses can often be planned and carried out by two teachers working together. High interventions can be discussed with your principal for suggestions of who might help.
3. In every instance that the response to the risk assessment questionnaire has triggered a suggested intervention (one of the three listed areas of concern), it is strongly recommended that you make at least a low response, which typically means a one-to-one interview with the student.
4. Low interventions will suggest an individual meeting or interview with the student to gather more information. Suggestions for discussion will be offered later in this manual. The low interview will help to ascertain whether medium or high interventions might also be beneficial.

5. Medium interventions may suggest ongoing support to monitor the student's situation. Typically you should discuss a medium intervention with another teacher who can help you develop a plan to help the student.

6. Your principal may suggest that when you have a student with high need for interventions you may ask a resource person for some help.

7. It is important for educators to use their knowledge and experience in interpreting the student responses during a one-on-one interview.

For example, question 1 asks, How often is the student angry? The responses include "never," "sometimes," "frequently," and "very frequently." What one student considers frequently may seem to peers and teachers to be very frequently, or, on the other hand, to be only sometimes. It all depends on the student's frame of reference. In deciding what level of intervention is necessary, it is helpful to look at what you know of—and can learn about—the student.

Appendix D

Dropout and Substance Abuse Prevention Proposal

SPECIFIC AIMS

The aims of project SAFE (Student/Staff and Family Education) are to develop a program model to: (1) identify risk factors for Hispanic students and families; (2) identify potential substance abusers and potential dropouts and gang affiliates; and (3) use an expert system to connect identified students with appropriate interventions which will reduce student risk levels.

The project goals are as follows:

Increase resiliency and protective factors with high-risk youth ages twelve to fourteen, their families, and the community to reduce the use of alcohol, drugs, and tobacco.

Reduce the risk factors for using alcohol, drugs, and tobacco with high-risk youth ages twelve to fourteen, their families, and the community.

Increase community agency's involvement in establishing a drug-free community.

Provide and field test alternative activities to use of alcohol, drugs, and tobacco for high-risk youth ages twelve to fourteen.

Develop a model for assisting inner-city Hispanic students and their parents in a community with strong gang involvement to resist drugs, alcohol, and tobacco usage.

Implement, evaluate and disseminate the SAFE project to create an adoptable/adaptable model to prevent abuse of alcohol, drugs, and tobacco in predominantly Hispanic communities for students ages twelve to fourteen.

The objectives of this project are as follows:

1. By September 200_, project participants will report a decrease in alcohol, tobacco and drug usage and gang affiliation.
2. By September 200_, students will report positive behavior responses to risk factors for using alcohol and other drugs as they impact on individual high-risk youth, and on the environments in which high-risk youths and their families function.
3. By September 200_, the majority of project students and parents will report an increase in the frequency of behaviors such as effectiveness in work, play and relationships; healthy expectations and a positive outlook; self-esteem and internal locus of control; self-discipline; problem solving; and critical thinking that reflect resiliency and protective factors for drug and alcohol usage.
4. By September 200_, there will be a significant statistical reduction among SAFE participants in the following school risk factors: academic failure, poor attendance, discipline referrals, and low commitment to school.
5. Annually, all project participants will be screened, identified and placed in the SAFE program.
6. Annually, an individual profile will be developed for project participants.
7. By September 200_, an individual profile will be perfected for distribution for clients ages twelve to fourteen who are at risk for alcohol, drug and/or tobacco use.
8. Annually, 90 percent of project participants will attend supervised school/community after-school activities that promote alternative activities to alcohol, drug, and tobacco use.
9. By September 200_, successful after-school activities for high-risk students will be written about in a publication based on evaluation reports in the project and the information disseminated.
10. By September 200_, project participants will report a reduction in alienation and rebelliousness, use of gateway drugs such as to-

bacco, peer associates who use drugs, alcohol, or tobacco, and an understanding of the health risk factors associated with usage.

11. By September 200_, participants will report improved family management, clear parental expectations, high expectations for personal success, and the benefits of healthy lifestyles.

12. Annually, teachers will receive training in prevention, detection, treatment of substance abuse, and self-esteem enhancement.

13. By September, 200_, linkages will be improved with the YMCA and Boys and Girls Clubs to provide alternative activities for high-risk youth involved in the SAFE program.

14. By September, 200_, a community network will be developed with assistance of United Way Agencies and Board of Directors to promote community involvement by increasing agency collaboration with schools, providing volunteers and mentors for school sites, and assisting in publicizing a no-use message.

15. By September 200_, a written plan will be developed with the Sheriff's Department and school district to coordinate project activities in drug prevention education and drug use intervention.

16. By September, 200_, a pamphlet will be developed and distributed in English and Spanish to explain signs and symptoms of alcohol and drug use and local agencies for treatment and assistance.

17. By September, 200_, a project dissemination/replication manual for the SAFE program will be available for distribution.

18. By September, 200_, the SAFE project will begin disseminating information to interested LEAs [local education agencies] through project SAFE manuals, conference presentations, and site visitations.

POPULATION TO BE SERVED AND TIME FRAME

This project will reach over eight hundred high-risk youth and their families over the five years of operation.

RATIONALE FOR PROJECT SUCCESS

This project is based on the research and models developed by Boyd and Howard[1] in the areas of health promotion, attachment, and bonding. The experience of Sunshine in working with high-risk youth in the areas of academics and school adjustments programs has been extensive.

NEEDS ASSESSMENT PROCESS

Sunshine School District's Substance Abuse Prevention Advisory was formed three years ago to determine the need for refinement and expansion of the existing Substance Abuse Prevention Program. The Advisory is now composed of the following: ten teachers and administrators representing all district schools; two law enforcement personnel; three parents, two from local businesses; and three from community counseling. The committee regularly reviews data from local and state agencies (Los Angeles County Sheriff, Office of Criminal Justice, California State Attorney General) on the frequency and severity of substance abuse among youth. The following highlights of that research indicate tragic proportions of the drug abuse problem: by age eleven, 11.7 percent of students report being intoxicated at least once; by age sixteen, 52 percent reported being intoxicated at least once; 40 percent of the students by age eight reported experimenting with drugs; 7.4 percent of eleventh graders reported daily use of marijuana, 39.3 percent of eleventh graders reported engaging in the extremely dangerous practice of using two or more drugs at the same time during the last six months. The Advisory also looked at those behaviors and factors that place students "at risk" for substance abuse. Results on a review of records and needs assessment surveys completed by staff and parents showed that over 37 percent K–12 students showed problems with chronic school failure, discipline, attendance, were children of alcoholics, and/or were educationally disadvantaged, among other factors. Also, over 60 percent of the students had no skills to cope with peer pressure advocating substance abuse.

Immigrant parents do not understand the criminal justice and/or the educational system. Parents, when confronted with the legal system, lack trust and understanding of how the system works. They often come from a country where law enforcement and government institutions are corrupt. They need education about the legal system, juvenile justice system, law enforcement, and the expectations of American institutions in general. In a telephone survey conducted by the district, 97 percent of parents support curriculum instructing students on the dangers of drugs and alcohol, 50 percent of parents were unaware of counseling programs, 61 percent were unaware of gang prevention programs, 45 percent were unaware of parenting classes, 40 percent were unaware of the drug education program, 80 percent were unaware of the drop-out prevention program, 72 percent were not involved in community groups. Some 54 percent were aware of district committees, but only 2 percent participated. Ninety-two (92 percent) of the parents surveyed approved of district programs. This gives evidence that parents need assistance in getting more involved in their children's education, but frequently do not know how because of cultural and linguistic differences.

As a result of this needs assessment, the Sunshine School District is implementing a highly successful curriculum-based K–12 Substance Abuse Prevention Program funded from the District's general fund and from the Drug-Free Schools and Communities Program. While this program has been successful in reducing substance abuse, especially at school, local needs assessment and research indicate there is a significant need for prevention programs focusing on high-risk youth, parent education, and a community-based campaign.

The Sunshine SAFE Program offers a comprehensive holistic approach for preventing alcohol and other drug use by students, in particular those at high risk, and is being evaluated over a period of five years. The project addresses the needs of the student, his family, the school, and community, in a comprehensive approach to prevention, through the following:

Student:
Identification of behavioral and academic deficits, and provision for peer tutoring, support group, and social skills and health curriculum;
An increase in social skills, peer resistance strategies, decision-making skills, and self-esteem;
An increase of bonding to home and school, with positive role models
An increase in academic performance and confidence in interacting with peers at school and home;
A decrease in antisocial behaviors.

School:
An increase in prevention knowledge, skills, and curriculum among teachers, counselors, and administrators;

Sensitization of staff to students' problems;

Providing a new dimension of health allowing more challenging physical fitness programs for risk-taking youth and providing extracurricular activities;

Providing a comprehensive program to address cognitive, social, health, personality concerns, as well as providing curriculum and materials;

Addressing family needs for parenting skills and drug prevention education;

Providing prevention specialists who interact with high-risk students, parents, and community.

Community:

Prevention Committee from schools, parents, police, health agencies meet quarterly to reinforce an antidrug use message for students;

The spirit of unity and responsibility strengthened and expanded by this concerted effort to prevent youth from experimenting with substances;

Businesses cooperating in offering time, jobs and services.

Family:

The need for better family management techniques and parenting skills being met through Neighborhood Watch and Active Parenting classes;

Parents gaining knowledge about drug use and ways to cope with children who have problems or are using;

Circle of Warmth meetings provided for at-risk parents;

Parents who need resources given help and support.

Students-at-Risk, Inc., will work with the school district to match interventions with a computerized high-risk profile of students called Comprehensive Risk Assessment. The software will be designed to use the many dropout and drug prevention interventions developed with potential substance-abusing students. A variety of media, including laser disks, films, videotapes, and interactive computer managed instruction will be used to deliver the instruction. The technical aspect will be low in cost to operate and will focus on an area, substance abuse prevention, that is in great demand in school districts throughout the nation.

It is apparent that a large number of school districts would be interested in a delivery system that addresses two of their most critical problems, students who use drugs and alcohol and students who are likely to drop out of school. It seems likely that we will have products which can do this, in that much of this work is already accomplished. What is more difficult to achieve is effective implementation of the delivery system. We will work diligently to accomplish this during the funding period. The identification software will not only serve to predict potential abusers and dropouts; it can serve as a means for evaluation of the effectiveness of prevention programs.

DROPOUT/DRUG/GANG PREVENTION CURRICULUM

The Sunshine Unified School District is committed to combat the ongoing problem of dropout and alcohol and other drug abuse on campuses and in the community at large. In addition, the district is a leader in the reduction of gang activity in schools. Many district administrators are called upon to make presentations throughout the region and state to faculties and professional organizations in the areas of at-risk students and drug and alcohol use and gang affiliation. These presentations have been made at the Superintendent's Academies, for the Association of California School Administrators, the Los Angeles County Office of Education, and for numerous other professional organizations.

The district has an adopted self-esteem program that is used preschool–12. The programs Magic Circle (PK–6) and Yo Puedo (I Can 7–12) are delivered to every student daily in Spanish and English. A companion program Circle of Warmth/Circulo de Carino is provided for parents. In addition to wellness lessons daily, each student participates in twenty hours of drug prevention each year through a partnership with the Los Angeles County Sheriff's Office in grades 4–6. Other grade levels receive instruction with the Here's Looking at You 2000 program in English and Spanish. This instruction includes social skills training using an assertive communication model and health concepts that promote health-enhancing behavior.

Sunshine School District has been recognized for its efforts in meeting the needs of high-risk youth. The school district has initiated and maintained a store-front program for dropout students called Youth Connection. Outreach counseling programs are available in Spanish and English for families of students preschool through high school. The district operates a pregnant minors program called GENESIS that serves the needs of young parents, their children, and pregnant minors. Groupings for school success are provided to students at every level. Teachers have been specially trained to meet the needs of students of all ages. The district superintendent, board members, and administrators have met and established an action plan for gang and drug reduction efforts. An outdoor adventure course is available and used to teach noncompetitive problem solving. At the center of every program is the goal of working with the whole family. With the addition of this grant, programs will be expanded to include the home and community using interventions based on the "Health Promotion," "Transformations," and "Social Development" models.

Using lottery funds, extra resources are provided to help the school staff create a dynamic and innovative center in an area of curriculum instruction. The program focuses staff energies on a specific area of special interest, promotes risk-taking and research, rewards collaboration rather than competition, and produces many sources of internal expertise throughout the district.

The Sunshine School District is committed to the implementation and continuation of this Holistic Substance Abuse Prevention Program. During the 1987–1988 school year, Sunshine School District implemented a comprehensive K–12 curriculum-based drug prevention program with district general funds and Drug-Free Schools and community funds. While this program has been successful in reducing substance abuse — especially at school, local needs assessment and research indicate there is a significant need to identify those factors that impact linguistic- and ethnic-divergent students and create a high-risk youth focus.

Sunshine School District has an exemplary record of working with "special needs" youth. They are recognized as a leader in servicing the needs of special education students. The district has pioneered consultative models of special education. Their multidisciplinary team approach to diagnosis and programming planning will be used as a component of project SAFE. Sunshine School District has met that challenge with extensive staff training and curriculum development.

IDENTIFICATION OF TARGET POPULATION

A coordinated intervention system that identifies high-risk juveniles or students from ethnic-/linguistic-divergent backgrounds with chronic drug abuse problems and gang affiliation and facilitates their referral to an established intervention system or drug abuse treatment program will be developed.

An alcohol and drug abuse prevention program will be provided to a total of 1,200 middle school students. An estimated 800 students will be identified yearly as high risk for developing drug abuse problems and gang affiliation. Twenty-five percent of the student population will be based on family alcohol risk characteristics. These high-risk students may be children of substance abusers and genetically at risk; students with low self-esteem; passive or aggressive students who are experiencing peer pressure problems; children who lack realistic information on destructive aspects of drugs; and children with behavioral or antisocial problems.

A high-risk student or one with a chronic drug abuse and/or gang affiliation problem is defined as a student having:

> problems with attendance, discipline, family, self-esteem, or academics; observed, reported, and/or self-reported substance abuse problems at school or in the community.

A data-gathering system involving students, parents, school personnel, and community resources to identify students who need help is being developed.

This project will implement an at-risk management system for the identification of students-at-risk and early intervention of school staff to assist youth who may become substance abusers and/or dropouts. Dr. Callison has extensive experience which will be helpful in the implementation of the at-risk management system. He has installed the personal computer version of the identification system in more than a dozen other school districts.

We have utilized the latest research on risk factors for both substance abusers and dropouts to develop software for identification. We would like to expand the program to identify cultural/linguistic variables.

EVALUATION PLAN

The evaluation will determine the attainment of project objectives. Each objective has been designed to be measurable. There are two aspects of the evaluation design for this program. Two forms of evaluation will be conducted: product and process. The product evaluation will focus on the expected performance of the participants. The process evaluation will be designed to monitor the completion of activities which support each objective and to facilitate replication if the approach proves promising.

NOTE

1. Gayle M. Boyd and Jan Howard, *Alcohol Problems among Adolescents: Current Directions in Prevention Research*, National Institute on Alcohol Abuse and Alcoholism, Michigan State University (Hillsdale, N.J.: Erlbaum, 1995).

Appendix E

How to Help Teachers Set Up a Homework Club

A change in attitude, in expectation, in beliefs, and in operation is necessary to accomplish the goals and objectives established for our school site. Every education employee at our site, including site administrator, teacher, instructional aide, and resource teacher, must intensify efforts to make this happen, and therefore, specific strategies must be developed and implemented to ensure that all students have an opportunity to succeed as they go through the education system.

This intervention program specifically addresses the needs of identified Chapter I students at Waterloo Elementary School in the Newton Unified School District—students whose achievement has been historically low, students primarily from minority communities. The district does not always provide adequately for these students to have equal access and academic achievement in the curriculum, and therefore this problem needs to be addressed through more detailed efforts to educate disenfranchised students through alternative extended day activities which supplement regular classroom instruction.

The following steps were followed to set up this after-school program.

1. The district staff expressed desire for the development of extended day programs to supplement Chapter I–funded activities.
2. The site administrator supports any activity that helps gain visibility and credibility for the school and that enhances the regular instructional program.

3. Teaching staff verbalized their frustration with students who have little or no success in the regular classroom.

4. Instructional aides stated that they want to learn how to better assist minority students in the regular classroom.

5. Parents indicated through informal conferences, parent teacher meetings, and family nights that they want their children to succeed academically and to develop basic study skills that help achieve success.

6. The resource teacher wants to respond to the need and requested permission to develop and conduct a test program that may serve as a model and potentially be adopted by other sites.

7. Current test scores for Chapter I–identified students are consistently low at this school site; the site administrator is concerned about this problem.

The administrator must determine what change situations and resultant problems are most prominent in his or her organization setting.

Administrative staff includes the district staff, site administrator, and the resource teacher, who, with a project partner from the outside, will play the most active role in implementing this change.

They determined change is needed to provide extended day activities which supplement core curriculum in regular classroom instruction, which enhances academic achievement in a language and culturally enriched environment at grade levels 4 to 6. This change will take place at the school site level. If successful, this intervention will be viewed as a pilot program for implementation at the district level.

- In assessing current resources and constraints on-site, it was determined that physical space is limited, and therefore only a small group of students can be accommodated by the extended day program this year.

- The site administrator is committed to supporting participation in an extended day program by the resource teacher, teaching staff, instructional aides, students, and parents.

- Teachers expressed frustration with students who are not performing well academically and who are experiencing language difficulties in the classroom, and requested assistance from the resource teacher.

- Parents were informally and formally polled about the study habits of their children to determine areas of need.
- Identified Chapter I students were given a Homework Assessment Survey, the results of which were used to target thirty to thirty-five program participants.
- District staff will support the program due to pressure for new program development. There are currently no other extended day programs of this type established for these grade levels within the district. The district needs a model of success that can be applied to other sites at little cost in implementation.
- The site administrator will support programs that address low academic achievement, low self-esteem of students, and allows for parent participation.
- Teaching staff may or may not support the program depending upon the level of their input, time, and effort required to assess students and to target them. In addition, some teachers are fundamentally opposed to Chapter I programs and do not want to participate or cooperate with the resource teacher.
- Instructional aides will support the program because they want to have a more direct role with the students, especially working with children with learning and language difficulties.
- Parents will support the program because they want their children to succeed academically, to like school, and to develop good study habits. In addition, many parents like the idea of extended day activities because it relieves the "latchkey kid" syndrome by provision of after-school care under adult supervision.

Organizational members may perform various roles related to change. The selecting of the most appropriate role is often determined by personal values and goals and/or organizational values and goals. The administrator may perform a variety of roles related to change.

Initiator: The resource teacher and her partner proposed the program after learning of the district's need for a model.

Stimulator: District staff envision that all school sites would have some type of extended day activity utilizing categorical funds.

Reactor: The site administrator approved the project and encouraged staff to support it.

Implementor: The resource teacher, her partner, teachers, and other site staff as assigned will conduct the surveys, assess results, set up parent education training, and develop curriculum for the program. Further, they will provide ongoing input and direct instructional support.

Conduit: The resource teacher is in the best strategic position to serve as conduit among administrative, and teaching staff, aides, parents, and students, especially as it relates to program objectives, parameters, needs, and progress. To a lesser degree, the site administrator will relay information to district staff.

Orchestrator-mediator: The site administrator and resource teacher will share the responsibility for ensuring that all parties fulfill their designated responsibilities.

Persuader or dissuader: The resource teacher and the site administrator are key persuaders in promoting the advantages of such a program to others.

Some teaching staff may serve as dissuaders by not wanting to philosophically support Chapter I programs, and by not wanting to take on additional responsibility to assist with targeting students and monitoring effects over time.

Advocate: The resource teacher, site administrator, and parents will serve as primary advocates for the program.

Ombudsman: Clerical and instructional aide staff can serve as ombudsmen, as a barometer for feedback from all parties involved, especially the students who participate in the program.

Nonactor: Some teaching staff will serve as nonactors, simply noting the changes that have occurred in student behavior and performance, attendance, parent involvement, and academic test scores.

IMPLEMENTATION PLAN

1. Discuss intervention and assessment tools with mentor, and obtain approval.
2. Share intervention outline with staff, parents, and site administrator. Obtain input and make adjustments accordingly.
3. Initiate process to complete a student homework assessment tool. Allow for time and opportunities to assist parents with draft format.

4. Target and select a group of thirty to thirty-five identified Chapter I students from information obtained from assessment tool.

5. Plan parent education training sessions with community liaison and site administrator.

6. Plan Family Night activities with assigned staff members, site administrator, and other community resource persons.

7. Meet with staff to align homework policies and assignments with extended day activities.

8. Schedule student orientation for Homework Club, Junior Achievement, and Be a Better Student seminars.

9. Analyze student homework assessment tool to align other curriculum to extended day activities.

10. Schedule meetings/conferences with teachers and other staff in regard to student progress.

11. Compare pre– and post–student homework assessment tool scores.

12. Assess intervention program results.

CONCLUSION

Primary intervention objectives were to build study skills, increase academic performance and self esteem of the students who participated, and increase parent participation in the school and in the home. This intervention program was successful in accomplishing these objectives.

The program proved to be an effective method to empower those directly involved in the educational process at this site and in addition, provided parents with an opportunity to be involved in a new and different way as an adult "mentor" to their own child. This included treating the child with respect; setting example for their improvement; monitoring and helping with homework; reading with the child; and keeping the school informed about the child's progress via a student homework assessment tool and Family Nights. The parents served as the primary link between the school and home. The program provided the framework, guidelines, and curriculum that help supplement and enhance the work of the school.

Attendance by parents of program participants reflected an average increase of 40 percent at school meetings and family nights; and other interactions with the school. Parents expressed increased satisfaction with the teaching taking place through the extended day activities. In addition, children and parents spent more time together, and children were more inclined to complete their homework assignments. Teaching staff attested to this through both quantitative and qualitative means.

In regard to academic achievement, preliminary data at midyear indicate student performance on standardized achievement tests will increase with 20 percent of the program participants scoring above the 35th percentile in Math and Reading, as compared to 5 percent of remaining Chapter I students who did not participate in the extended day activities.

As a result of the program, students were less reluctant to join in other school activities, both academic and social. They appeared to take on more leadership roles with ease. Many of them served as a catalyst within their home to increase family participation at school functions. Students were less intimidated by homework assignments, and the school structure and bureaucracy. They developed more personal relationships with various school staff, such as the resource teacher, librarian, and instructional aides.

Student commitment to academics improved as attendance records for the first semester reflected a 90 percent attendance rate in the extended day program.

The program helped to build a broader network of site staff and the family community in support of education. It encouraged parents to use existing school services and resources, and identified new ways for them to support their children. Parents took a role in sharing the school vision, participated in implementing the school plan, and evaluated the progress of meeting the objectives in the school plan. Parent observations were used in decision making.

Ultimately, this intervention program recognized the important link among meaningful parent education, parent involvement, culturally and language-enriched extended day activities, and improved academic achievement. The school served as a bridge to the district and the community by serving as a resource to the families, students, and other school sites within the district with similar Chapter I populations.

Appendix F

National Standards for Parent/ Family Involvement Programs

COMMUNICATION BETWEEN HOME AND SCHOOL IS REGULAR, TWO-WAY, AND MEANINGFUL

Communication is the foundation of a solid partnership. When parents and educators communicate effectively, positive relationships develop, problems are more easily solved, and students make greater progress.

Too often school or program communication is one way without the chance to exchange ideas and share perceptions. Effective home-school communication is the two-way sharing of information vital to student success. Even parent–teacher conferences can be one way if the goal is merely reporting student progress. Partnering requires give-and-take conversation, goal setting for the future, and regular follow-up interactions.

Quality Indicators

Successful programs:

1. Use a variety of communication tools on a regular basis, seeking to facilitate two-way interaction through each type of medium.
2. Establish opportunities for parents and educators to share partnering information such as student strengths and learning preferences.

Excerpted with permission from National PTA's National Standards for Parent/Family Involvement Programs, © 1998.

3. Provide clear information regarding course expectations and offerings, student placement, school activities, student services, and optional programs.
4. Mail report cards and regular progress reports to parents. Provide support services and follow-up conferences as needed.
5. Disseminate information on school reforms, policies, discipline procedures, assessment tools, and school goals, and include parents in any related decision-making process.
6. Conduct conferences with parents at least twice a year, with follow-up as needed. These should accommodate the varied schedules of parents, language barriers, and the need for child care.
7. Encourage immediate contact between parents and teachers when concerns arise.
8. Distribute student work for parental comment and review on a regular basis.
9. Translate communications to assist non-English-speaking parents.
10. Communicate with parents regarding positive student behavior and achievement, not just regarding misbehavior or failure.
11. Provide opportunities for parents to communicate with principals and other administrative staff.
12. Promote informal activities at which parents, staff, and community members can interact.
13. Provide staff development regarding effective communication techniques and the importance of regular two-way communication between the school and the family.

Program Orientation

At the beginning of the school or program year, offer orientation sessions that include the following:

- Course or program expectations and goals
- Developmental and skills information
- Information on how/when to contact program staff or administration
- Process for handling program questions/concerns
- Strategies to support learning at home
- Testing/assessment information and procedures

Always include a time for questions and answers to address specific parent or family concerns. If possible, provide a video recording of the event to share with those unable to attend.

Building Partnerships

With so many students, how can educators build effective partnerships with each of their parents? One teacher sets aside 10 minutes a day to telephone, e-mail, or send postcards to parents. Once a month the teacher is able to make at least two contacts with each family represented in the class. Most conversations focus on student successes and upcoming activities for parents and families. Because of the consistent contact and accessibility, parents are more eager to respond and support student/class goals.

Sample Applications

Use a Variety of Communication Tools

- Explore program and community support options for improving mail, telephone, fax, or e-mail access and use for educators and parents. For example, automated phone systems are a powerful tool for getting information to parents—from daily assignments and attendance reports to parenting tips and student achievement information.
- Create class or program newsletters for parents that contain tips for helping children learn in the home, fun activities to do as a family, and other useful ideas.
- Establish a routine method for parents to review their children's work on a regular basis. For example, use manila envelopes or folders to send student work home each week with a place for parent comments on the front cover.
- Implement additional feedback opportunities for parents and family members such as surveys on current program issues or special parent guest columns in the school newsletter.
- Sponsor program or community events that allow educators and parents to interact on a social basis in addition to standard parent–teacher conferences or school/program meetings.

- Develop a parent handbook to provide positive, practical information about your school or program. Include information on how parents can support their child's efforts to succeed.

PARENTING

Parents are a child's life support system. Consequently, the most important support a child can receive comes from the home.

School personnel and program staff support positive parenting by respecting and affirming the strengths and skills needed by parents to fulfill their role. From making sure that students arrive at school rested, fed, and ready to learn, to setting high learning expectations and nurturing self-esteem, parents sustain their children's learning.

When staff members recognize parent roles and responsibilities, ask parents what supports they need, and work to find ways to meet those needs, they communicate a clear message to parents: "We value you and need your input" in order to maintain a high-quality program.

Quality Indicators

Successful programs:

1. Communicate the importance of positive relationships between parents and their children.
2. Link parents to programs and resources within the community that provide support services to families.
3. Reach out to all families, not just those who attend parent meetings.
4. Establish policies that support and respect family responsibilities, recognizing the variety of parenting traditions and practices within the community's cultural and religious diversity.
5. Provide an accessible parent/family information and resource center to support parents and families with training, resources, and other services.
6. Encourage staff members to demonstrate respect for families and the family's primary role in the rearing of children to become responsible adults.

RESPECTING DIVERSE FAMILY CULTURES AND TRADITIONS

Quality schools and programs must be culturally sensitive to increasingly diverse student and family populations. Appreciating the traditions of families from various cultures requires, first of all, an awareness and acceptance of their differences.

Find ways to help parents and families value and share their distinctiveness. Cultural fairs or other opportunities to celebrate specific ethnic holidays or traditions may help parents and family members develop a sense of belonging and ownership in the school and community. Making resources available in the parents' first language remains critical in responding to the needs and concerns of the parents and families served.

Parent and Family Resource Centers

Designate an area in your school or community for parents and family members to call their own. The "center" should be tailored to respond to the issues and concerns of your school or program members.

The center's function could vary from providing an informal gathering place for parents to share information, to providing comprehensive access to community services. A wide array of family resource and support materials including videos, brochures, and other publications are often included. Some centers have expanded to provide parenting workshops, toy-lending libraries, or English as a Second Language (ESL) classes.

Highlighting "what's new at the family center" in each school newsletter and sponsoring special family or education events at the center throughout the year helps to increase the center's visibility and effectiveness.

Quality Indicators

Parents play an integral role in assisting student learning.

Student learning increases when parents are invited into the process by helping at home. Enlisting parents' involvement provides educators and administrators with a valuable support system—creating a team that is working for each child's success.

The vast majority of parents are willing to assist their students in learning, but many times are not sure what assistance is most helpful and appropriate. Helping parents connect to their children's learning enables parents to communicate in powerful ways that they value what their children achieve. Whether it's working together on a computer, displaying student work at home, or responding to a particular class assignment, parents' actions communicate to their children that education is important.

Successful programs:

1. Seek and encourage parental participation in decision making that affects students.
2. Inform parents of the expectations for students in each subject at each grade level.
3. Provide information regarding how parents can foster learning at home, give appropriate assistance, monitor homework, and give feedback to teachers.
4. Regularly assign interactive homework that will require students to discuss and interact with their parents about what they are learning in class.
5. Sponsor workshops or distribute information to assist parents in understanding how students can improve skills, get help when needed, meet class expectations, and perform well on assessments.
6. Involve parents in setting student goals each year and in planning for post-secondary education and careers. Encourage the development of a personalized education plan for each student, where parents are full partners.
7. Provide opportunities for staff members to learn and share successful approaches to engaging parents in their child's education.

How Much Help Is Too Much?

Offer suggestions to parents on how they can help their children learn, including questions to ask and practical ways to practice skills. One English teacher describes how parents can ask questions and make suggestions to help students learn and practice writing skills. Studies have found that writing improves when students seek advice from others and write for an audience. Parents and family members can provide that needed feedback and support.

Student–Parent Workshops

Provide brief workshops on specific topics of interest to students and parents. Topics might include a series on study skills, new information on a particular curriculum area such as math or science, or college and career planning. When applicable, include hands-on learning activities and detailed information to help both parents and students practice new skills.

Sample Home-to-School Communication

Design homework assignments to include parent sign-off. Provide instructions about what to look for in each assignment, and offer a quick check-off response such as:

[ ] My child understands and correctly applies this skill.
[ ] My child needed help on this, but overall seems to understand this lesson.
[ ] My child needs further instruction on this skill/lesson.
Other comments _____
Parent signature _____

VOLUNTEERING

Parents are welcome in the school, and their support and assistance are sought.

When parents volunteer, both families and schools reap benefits that come in few other ways. Literally millions of dollars of volunteer services are performed by parents and family members each year in the public schools. Studies have concluded that volunteers express greater confidence in the schools where they have opportunities to participate regularly. In addition, assisting in school or program events/activities communicates to a child, "I care about what you do here."

In order for parents to feel appreciated and welcome, volunteer work must be meaningful and valuable to them. Capitalizing on the expertise and skills of parents and family members provides much needed support to educators and administrators already taxed in their attempts to meet academic goals and student needs.

Although there are many parents for whom volunteering during school hours is not possible, creative solutions like before- or after-school "drop-in" programs or "at home" support activities provide opportunities for parents to offer their assistance as well.

Quality Indicators

Successful programs:

1. Ensure that office staff greetings, signage near the entrances, and any other interaction with parents create a climate in which parents feel valued and welcome.
2. Survey parents regarding their interests, talents, and availability, then coordinate the parent resources with those that exist within the school and among the faculty.
3. Ensure that parents who are unable to volunteer in the school building are given the options for helping in other ways, at home, or place of employment.
4. Organize an easy, accessible program for utilizing parent volunteers, providing ample training on volunteer procedures and school protocol.
5. Develop a system for contacting all parents to assist as the year progresses.
6. Design opportunities for those with limited time and resources to participate by addressing child care, transportation, work schedule needs, and so forth
7. Show appreciation for parents' participation, and value their diverse contributions.
8. Educate and assist staff members in creating an inviting climate and effectively utilizing volunteer resources.
9. Ensure that volunteer activities are meaningful and built on volunteer interests and abilities.

Volunteer Orientation

Take time to train volunteers regarding school or program protocols, routines and procedures, volunteer expectations, and equipment usage. In addition, provide a central location for volunteers to work with secure places for personal belongings.

Give clear instructions for completing volunteer tasks as well as the appropriate staff or teacher contact name if more information is needed. Look for creative ways to show appreciation for volunteer support on an ongoing basis.

Volunteer Information Packet

As part of the volunteer orientation, provide a packet containing the following important information:

Accident procedures
Building map
Emergency exit plans
Equipment operating instructions
Parking information
School or program handbook
Sign-in/ -out policies
Suggestion forms
Volunteer welcome letter and list of benefits
Volunteer work locations
Where to go for help and supplies

SCHOOL DECISION MAKING AND ADVOCACY

Parents are full partners in the decisions that affect children and families.

Studies have shown that schools where parents are involved in decision making and advocacy have higher levels of student achievement and greater public support.

Effective partnerships develop when each partner is respected and empowered to fully participate in the decision-making process. Schools and programs that actively enlist parent participation and input communicate that parents are valued as full partners in the educating of their children.

Parents and educators depend on shared authority in decision-making systems to foster parental trust, public confidence, and mutual support of each other's efforts in helping students succeed. The involvement of parents, as individuals or as representatives of others, is crucial in collaborative decision-making processes on issues from curriculum and course selection, to discipline policies and over-all school reform measures.

Quality Indicators

Successful programs:

1. Provide understandable, accessible, and well-publicized processes for influencing decisions, raising issues or concerns, appealing decisions, and resolving problems.
2. Encourage the formation of PTAs or other parent groups to identify and respond to issues of interest to parents.
3. Include parents on all decision-making and advisory committees, and ensure adequate training for such areas as policy, curriculum, budget, school reform initiatives, safety, and personnel. Where site governance bodies exist, give equal representation to parents.
4. Provide parents with current information regarding school policies, practices, and both student and school performance data.
5. Enable parents to participate as partners when setting school goals, developing or evaluating programs and policies, or responding to performance data.
6. Encourage and facilitate active parent participation in the decisions that affect students, such as student placement, course selection, and individual personalized education plans.
7. Treat parental concerns with respect and demonstrate genuine interest in developing solutions.
8. Promote parent participation on school district, state, and national committees and issues.
9. Provide training for staff and parents on collaborative partnering and shared decision making.

Parent Involvement in Making Program Decisions

By recruiting parent representatives to serve on committees dealing with policies and program decisions, administrators acknowledge the importance of parents' knowledge of and experience with children.

To ensure ongoing effective parent participation in the decision-making process, policy makers can work to create an environment where parents can:

- Attend open meetings on school/program issues
- Receive clear program goals and objectives

- Ask questions without fear of intimidation
- Understand confusing terminology and jargon
- Monitor the steps taken to reach program goals
- Assist their children in understanding program expectations and changes

Volunteer Information Packet

Promoting positive, constructive parent advocacy begins with frequently publicizing the process for dealing with concerns.

Parents need to understand the steps to problem solving and feel that the administration is genuinely interested in responding to their concerns in a constructive and fair manner.

The process should include identifying the problem, keeping the focus on the student's needs, avoiding blaming, meeting with the proper person(s) involved, gathering pertinent facts and information, brainstorming potential solutions, developing an action plan, and implementing and checking on progress. Repeat each step as necessary to resolve the problem.

COLLABORATING WITH COMMUNITY

Community resources are used to strengthen schools, families, and student learning.

As part of the larger community, schools and other programs fulfill important community goals. In like fashion, communities offer a wide array of resources valuable to schools and the families they serve.

When schools and communities work together, both are strengthened in synergistic ways and make gains that outpace what either entity could accomplish on its own:

- Families access community resources more easily.
- Businesses connect education programs with the realities of the workplace.
- Seniors contribute wisdom and gain a greater sense of purpose.
- Students serve and learn beyond their school involvement.

The best partnerships are mutually beneficial and structured to connect individuals, not just institutions or groups. This connection enables the power of community partnerships to be unleashed.

Quality Indicators

Successful programs:

1. Distribute information regarding cultural, recreational, academic, health, social, and other resources that serve families within the community.
2. Develop partnerships with local business and service groups to advance student learning and assist schools and families.
3. Encourage employers to adopt policies and practices that promote and support adult participation in children's education.
4. Foster student participation in community service.
5. Involve community members in school volunteer programs.
6. Disseminate information to the school community, including those without school-age children, regarding school programs and performance.
7. Collaborate with community agencies to provide family support services and adult learning opportunities, enabling parents to more fully participate in activities that support education.
8. Inform staff members of the resources available in the community and strategies for utilizing those resources.

EMPLOYER SUPPORT

Innovative businesses have established policies that enable parents to support their children's learning more easily. Some are allowing parents to adjust work schedules to attend parent-teacher conferences or serve as volunteers. Other employers distribute school and program information or recognize employees who give personal time to support schools.

Within each community is a unique mix of organizations and service agencies that can offer valuable support to parents and families. Consider the following partner categories:

Businesses
Chamber of Commerce
Charitable organizations
Churches
Civic groups
Foundations
Local government
Local media
Military groups
Nonprofit associations
Senior citizens
Youth groups

COMMUNITY SERVICE LEARNING

More and more schools are providing students with the opportunity to learn by serving in the community. From soup kitchens and clean-up projects to volunteer activities in government and business, these hands-on student opportunities are especially powerful when linked to class discussions and curriculum objectives. In some cases where student skills have been linked to employee needs, not only have employers expanded opportunities for student learning, but their companies have also benefited. Through these programs, employers are able to complete important projects, while students benefit from new learning experiences in actual work settings.

Index

About the Author

William L. Callison has been deeply involved in the parent involvement program of the Even Start Program in the Bakersfield (California) City (Elementary) School District as the evaluator for three years. Even Start is primarily a program for low-income parents built around the assumption that the best way to help young children (three-year-olds in this program) to prepare for school is to have mothers bring their children to a two-hour morning program five days a week, forty-five weeks a year. The children prepare for kindergarten, and the mothers learn to read and to take care of their children. The mothers also are working to pass the GED high school equivalency examination.

He has also been involved in the creation of the Head Start Supplementary Training Program, which he then served as national director. This parent training effort has operated since 1966 and involves scores of small staff and parent groups in every state as they learn to be teacher aides in Head Start classrooms.

Callison is emeritus professor of educational leadership at California State University at Fullerton and holds a Ph.D. from Stanford.